ENCYCLOPAEDIA OF WOMEN IN SOUTH ASIA (MALDIVES)

ENCYCLOPAEDIA
OF
WOMEN IN SOUTH ASIA

(In 8 Volumes)

Maldives

(Volume 8)

Editors

Sangh Mittra, Bachchan Kumar

KALPAZ PUBLICATIONS

Delhi-110052

Encyclopaedia of Women in South Asia *(Maldives)*
(International Studies, Women)

Rs. 7000 (Set)

ISBN: 81-7835-187-0 (Set)
ISBN: 81-7835-195-1 (Vol. 8)

Published in 2004 in India by
Kalpaz Publications,
C-30, Satyawati Nagar, Delhi-110052
E-mail : Kalpaz@hotmail.com

Laser Typesetting at : Shree Vaishnavi Creations, Delhi
Printed at : Mehra Offset Press, Delhi

Contents

1

Historical Background, Geography and People

The Maldive islands are situated in south-west of India, on both sides of the equator. The islands are numerous the people are small, adapted to island life where main nutrition is fish, coconuts and imported rice. The total population of the 1,200 islands is about 270,000. The nation living in the Maldive islands has been isolated from the outside world for much of its history. The only contacts to other people have been through sea-trade, which is also the route Islam found its way to the islands. Maldives comprises some 1,200 islands in the Indian Ocean. Originally Buddhists, Maldivians were converted to Sunni Islam in the mid-12th century. Islam is the official religion of nearly the entire population. Strict adherence to Islamic precepts and close community relationships have helped keep crime under control.

The common language as well as the official language is Dhivehi, an Indo-European language related to Sinhala, the language of Sri Lanka. The writing system, like Arabic, is from right to left, although alphabets are different. English is used widely in commerce and increasingly as the medium of instruction in government schools.

The Maldivian economy is predominantly based on tourism and fishing. Of 1,200 islands, only 198 are inhabited. The population is scattered throughout the country, and the greatest concentration is on the capital island, the development has been centered upon the tourism industry, transport, distribution, real estate, construction, and government. Taxes on the tourist industry have been plowed into infrastructure and also used to improve technology in the agricultural sector.

The early records of Maldive throw light on female rulers and inheritance of power through female line. The present day society, however, is dominated by male clerics and an adapted Islamic code of conduct. Women still enjoy several rights compared to women in many other Islamic countries like equal rights to education and freedom in selecting and divorcing spouses. In fact the Maldive islands have been populated as early as historical records are available. Estimates based on archaeology and linguistics conclude that the islands were populated around 2,500 years ago if not earlier. The population has arrived in small quantities during a long period of time, and most probably it is a mixture of different groups, some of them coming from India and Sri Lanka, some from even farther as survivors of shipwrecks.

There is a reluctance, if not opposition in the Maldives to the study of early history. The unity of Islamic society seems to demand that - what they see as - the contemptible past before Islamic faith is forgotten. In practice, all artefacts preceding Islamic time have been systematically destroyed up to the present. The Moslem ban of idolatry has been followed literally. Still in 1988 the customs officials picked off Buddha-pictures which belonged to a UN expert.

Buddhism

There is archaeological evidence of Buddhist and Hindu worship in ancient times, which is natural taken the location of islands next to India and Sri Lanka. Thor Heyerdal suggests even earlier, different forms of worship but since his book The Maldive Mystery there has not been any research in that matter. There are numerous un-excavated ruins of temples and shrines on the islands.

The first historical records concerning the Maldives come from first centuries of our era. Clarence Maloney lists Sri Lankan, Greek, Indian, Chinese, Arab and European travellers as sources of information. One of the most complete descriptions of the Maldive Islands and their inhabitants can be found in the account of Ibn Battuta of his travels. He stayed in Male in 1344, and gives detailed information about the economy and society when it seems to have been at its peak.

Islam

Islam was introduced to the Maldives in the 12th century, and in 1155 the whole nation was converted after the decree of the king who took the title of Sultan. Old temples were demolished and mosques built on their foundations. The rites of new religion were followed from early times: ablutions and prayer-times, pilgrimage to Mecca and recital of the Quaran. Islamic law and moral codes were imposed upon the population much later, mainly in this century. Physical punishment used to be uncommon (as Ibn Battuta records) and women's dress light, not covering the upper body.

Up-to the 16th century there were several female rulers in Maldive. The succession on throne was given originally to the younger brothers of the king, and in absence of brothers, to a daughter and her sister like in Sri Lankan dynasties. This started to change to the direction of son following father, but it was never firmly established, and because of the unclear orders of succession there was much rivalry and numerous coup d'états. The strongest Sultana, Khadeeja, followed her father. Twice she was deposed by a husband, but both times she was able to overthrow and kill the treacherous husband, and finally her sister succeeded her to the throne, During her reign Male was a trade centre, and the royal court subsisted on imported rice. The Sultana had a foreign bodyguard of one thousand men. Maldives exported cowrie-shells (which were used as currency in a wide area), coconut products, fine cotton fabrics and copper-vessels. The level of handicrafts were unsurpassed at that time.

Ibn Battuta's Version

Excerpts from Ibn Battuta:

> Their womenfolk do not cover their heads, not even their queen does so, and they comb their hair and gather it at one side. Most of them wear only an apron from their waists to the ground, the rest of their bodies being uncovered. When I held the qadiship there, I tried to put an end to this practice and ordered them to wear clothes, but I met with no success. It is easy to get married on these islands on account on the smallness of the dowries and the pleasure of their women's society. When ships

arrive, the crew marry many wives, and when they are about to sail they divorce them. It is really a sort of temporary marriage. The women never leave their country. It is a strange thing about these islands that their ruler is a woman, Khadija. - Her army comprises about a thousand men, recruited from abroad, Though some are natives. ..they are paid in rice monthly. The first bad custom I changed (as a qadi) was the practice of divorced wives of staying in the houses of their former husbands, for they all do so till they marry another husband.

The kinship system could be originally matrilineal which means that family was traced along female line. Maloney uses linguistic material, anthropological material from the nearby Lakshadveep islands and from the coast of Kerala in India, and historical descriptions, and compares these to the traces found in the present society to prove this point.

The Nayars of Kerala were warriors and landowners. They lived in relatial houses called taravads, which was occupied by a matrilineal extended family. The titular head of the household was the great mother, but her brother was the manager of the household. They lived in the same taravad through their whole lives. Even married men just visited their wives overnight but returned to eat and work in their native taravad. There was a matriliny in inheritance as well.

In the Lakshadveep islands matriliny has survived until this century even though Islam is the religion. On the northern Maliku island which is closest to the Lakshadvip houses are inherited through female line and men have only the right of residence.

Women in Today's Society

Maldives is a low-income country where both fertility and mortality are high: average number of children born to one woman being seven. Infant and child mortality on some of the remote islands is very high, in worst cases only half of the children reach adulthood. A woman marries in average four times in her life. Divorces are common because Islam makes divorcing easy for the husband, and marriages are not considered as a family business but an individual choice.

Often people live in their birth homes, even married

couples may only visit each other. Or a woman may stay in her ex-husbands house after divorce together with her children. A child in the capital Male may tell to her teacher that on Friday she "went to park with my mother's children" meaning the children of her father's new wife. It has been estimated that the record of number of marriages for one couple is 99 - after every quarrel they divorced but then again married each other. Traditional beliefs in witchcraft are still strong. People are afraid of spirits, jinnies, which may come from the sea or live in trees. The so called Fandita men are specialists against bad jinnies and sicknesses. The capital Male' is a small island populated by over 60,000 people. The congestion is unbelievable, people live in small dark houses often without any yard or garden space, average 14 people and three families living in one house. The ground water is polluted, and in the dry season there are severe shortages of water. Some people have to sleep in shifts because there is not enough space or beds.

Women and kids mainly stay inside their living-quarters except upper- and middle-class women who are employed in clerical professions in offices. All manual labor except household chores is done by men. Men do most of the shopping and trading and spend time in tea-shops. Cooking takes a long time every day, and much time is spent in sitting and chatting with other women.

Tourism has greatly flourished in Maldive on account of its natural and scenic beauty. This has added to their affluence. Thus they can import foreign workers for manual labour to do construction. Hotel staff comes often from Philippines, and many teachers from Sri Lanka. 93% of Maldivians are literate but very few have secondary education. They have their own language Divehi which is related to the Indo-Aryan languages of India, and their own script. Higher studies are in English, however.

Impacts of Islamic Fundamentalism

Arabic countries have been financing the building of several new Mosques, and they rival of influence: both Kuwait, Libya and Iran have been donating funds for construction. The traditional dress of women on islands is one-coloured and simple but decorated with a colourful collar. In Male' women wear a covering though tight gown of shiny material, and government employees additionally a kerchief attached to hair. Women like to dress fancifully in glittering materials, and young women also wear Pakistani-style tunic-trouser-combination. Introduction of a head-cover and Arabic-style dress has been a recent phenomenon.

Girls who want to show that they are not vain and interested in only worldly matters like Indian music and movies but have a spiritual inner life, wear the scarf even though it is usually made of shiny white and bright-blue materials.

Women's Health Status

The expectancy of life and mortality rates are the most commonly used indicators of the health status of a population, in the absence of suitable measurements that can adequately capture the holistic meaning of health as defined by WHO. Life expectancy at birth is a hypothetical measure expressing the average number of years a newborn can be expected to live if the current mortality trends continue. It indicates the current health and mortality conditions in a population. Globally, the combined life expectancy at birth for both sexes increased from 46.5 years in 1950-55 to 64.3 years in 1990-95, an increase of 17.8 years. In the Region, six of the 10 countries (DPR Korea, India, Indonesia, Maldives, Myanmar and Thailand) have added 20 years or more to their life expectancies since 1950.

Communicable diseases remain the leading cause of death worldwide, killing at least 17 million people annually. The South-East Asia Region accounts for 41% of these deaths – almost 7 million deaths each year. This figure underestimates the impact of infectious diseases, since some noncommunicable diseases, such as malnutrition and cancer, can result from or be aggravated by infection.

The spectrum of infectious diseases is rapidly changing in conjunction with the dramatic socioeconomic and ecological changes taking place. Very little sex-specific data on the incidence and prevalence of some of the communicable diseases, such as tuberculosis, malaria and leprosy, were found for the Region. The literature examining the influence of gender on the risk of infection, prevalence and access to treatment of many commu-nicable diseases is also scanty.

Tuberculosis (TB) is an ancient disease which continues to pose a major public health challenge in developing countries. It is a bacterial infection caused by Mycobacterium tuberculosis (tubercle bacillus) and occa-sionally by Mycobacterium bovis and Mycobacterium africanum. Transmission of tuberculosis occurs mainly by airborne spread of infectious droplets.

Tuberculosis is a serious challenge because of its rapid spread in recent years, primarily due to coinfection with HIV/AIDS and the emergence of drug-resistant strains. Tuberculosis is reported to be the single leading infectious cause of death in women world-wide, killing over one million women every year, mainly bet-ween the ages of 15 and 44. Approximately half a million female deaths in the Region in 1997 were caused by TB. According to an epidemiological trend assessment of tuberculosis done for the period 1989-1993, 55% of the new cases reported annually were males and 45% were females throughout the five-year period . According to population-based surveys conducted in 119 randomly selected villages in Bangalore district in India between 1961 and 1968, there Sex differentials in the prevalence of tuberculosis may vary across age groups. According to population-based surveys conducted in 119 randomly selected villages in Bangalore district in India between 1961 and 1968, there was little difference by sex in tuberculosis prevalence rates up to the age of 14 years. After this age, the prevalence rates for males were from 20% to 70% higher than for females.

It is thus evident that when the overall annual risk of tuberculosis infection was high, women aged 15-35 years had higher tuberculosis notification rates than men in the same age group. This was the case in countries of Europe and America during the mid-twentieth cen-tury, when the overall annual risk of tuberculosis infection was as high as is currently the situation in many countries of the Region. It is possible then, that in countries of the Region, the lower prevalence of tuberculosis in women aged 15-35 years is the result of under-notification of infected women.

Very often women were victims of T.B. in large number according to data for the 15-year period from 1981-1994 compiled by the Registrar General of India. A 1976 study conducted in Nagpur, India found mortality rates (deaths due to tuberculosis in the population) to be slightly higher for females in the 5-14 year age group, and 10-36% higher for females in the 15-34 year age group. After the age of 35 years, men's mortality rates were several times higher. Thus the tuberculosis of the geni-tourinary tract, which is often difficult to diagnose, can cause infertility in women. This type of tuberculosis has potentially serious consequences for women's lives. A 1993 study in Darjeeling, India carried bacteriological and histological investigations of endometrial curettings of 800 non-pregnant women between 15 and 60 years of age. The women complained of infertility, abnormal uterine bleeding, amenorrhoea, leukorrhoea and other gynaecological problems. Social consequences on women affected by tuberculosis have been examined in some studies in India. A study in one district of Maharashtra found that conjugal families showed an inability or unwilling-ness to support the women.

According to another study in 1997, afflicted men worried about loss of wages, financial difficulties and reduced capacity for work performance at jobs, and consequences of long absence from work. Women had to worry about rejection by the husband, harassment by the in-laws and, if unmarried, reduced chances of marriage.

Tuberculosis is the most important life-threatening opportunistic infection associated with HIV infection in the South-East Asia Region. HIV infection and tuberculosis each speed up the progression of the other. Of the 5.5 million people who were estimated to be HIV positive in 1999, about one-third were also infected with tuberculosis. Between 56% and 80% of AIDS cases diagnosed in India, Myanmar, Nepal and Thailand have had tuberculosis. While HIV seroprevalence was found to be higher in female than in male tuberculosis patients in Africa, the converse is found in South-East Asia. A higher proportion of male as compared to female tuberculosis patients were found to be HIV positive in surveys of tuberculosis patients in Yangon, Myanmar. Although there was no information available from other countries of the Region, a similar pattern was also observed in Cambodia, with female and male HIV seropre-valence rates among tuberculosis patients of 2.5% and 5.2% respectively. The reason for this difference is unclear. One possible explanation is that the HIV epidemic in South-East Asia is at least a decade behind the African epidemic, and in the early stages of the epidemic more men than women have been found to be HIV infected.

A number of factors may contribute to women having poorer access than men to tuberculosis diagnostic services and to effective treatment. Among these are lack of time and resources and lack of decision-making power, which affect women's access to health services in general. More specific to care-seeking for tuberculosis, are poor knowledge of the disease and poor interpretation of its signs and symptoms by the women themselves as well as by the health workers, the social stigma associated with being diagnosed with tuberculosis, and the financial and time costs of the prolonged course of tuberculosis treatment.

Evidence of sex differentials in health seeking behaviour and utilisation of services is mixed. A study of 297 new sputum positive cases in Nepal found that women tended to delay seeking care much more than men. The mean reported duration of cough before diagnosis was 27 days for men as opposed to 49 days for women.

In Bangladesh, India and Nepal, there was no difference by sex in attendance of tuberculosis patients at general health facilities. In Hyderabad, India, while the sex ratio of patients seeking care in a private trust hospital was 1 male to 0.8 female, the sex ratio of patients referred by private practitioners was 1 male to 1 female, and that of patients referred by female private practitioners, 1 male to 2 females. This suggests that women tended to seek help from a female private practitioner when they first became aware of the need for treatment of their symptoms. While HIV seroprevalence was found to be higher in female than in male tuberculosis patients in Africa, the converse is found in South East Asia.

While some studies report a greater rate of compliance among women who do seek treatment, a meta-analysis of studies looking into gender differentials in treatment compliance suggests a more cautious interpretation. The compliance rates did not differ between men and women in 10 of the 15 studies included in the analysis. All the same, none of the studies showed a better compliance rate for male as compared to female patients.

HIV/AIDS and Women

Acquired immunodeficiency syndrome (AIDS) is caused

by the human immunodeficiency virus (HIV). HIV gradually breaks down the human body's natural defence mechanisms, making it vulnerable to infections and unable to fight off diseases. A person infected with HIV may not show any manifestation of AIDS for 7-10 years. Once AIDS is diagnosed, a person in a developing country setting may not survive for more than two years. More than 80% of infections in the South-East Asia Region are a result of heterosexual transmission. Other routes of transmission are through blood or blood products, donated semen or organs, or from an infected mother to her child. From a newly emergent and mysterious illness in the 1980s, AIDS rapidly evolved into a global pandemic in less than 20 years. Currently, an estimated 33 million adults and children are living with HIV/AIDS. Of the estimated 12 million deaths from AIDS since the beginning of the epidemic, 2.5 million occurred in 1998 alone. Although HIV infection was slower to emerge in South-East Asia than in other parts of the world, it is now a serious public health problem. The first AIDS case in the Region was diagnosed in Thailand in 1984.

Reproductive health, as defined by the World Health Organization and adopted by the Programme of Action of the International Conference on Population and Development (ICPD) means "... a state of complete physical, mental and social well-being and not merely the absence of disease or infirmity, in all matters relating to the reproductive system and to its functions and processes. Reproductive health therefore implies that people are able to have a satisfying and safe sex life and that they have the capability to reproduce and the freedom to decide if, when and how often to do so". The right to reproductive health is a key component of women's and men's reproductive and sexual rights. Moreover, the achievement of reproductive health is inextricably linked to women's and men's ability to exercise reproductive and sexual rights, which include, besides the right to reproductive health, the right to:

— reproductive decision-making including voluntary choice in marriage, family formation and determination of the num-ber, timing and spacing of one's children; and the right to have access to the information and means needed to exercise voluntary choice;

- equality and equity for men and women to enable individuals to make free and informed choices in all spheres of their life, free from discrimination based on gender;
- sexual and reproductive security including freedom from sexual violence and coercion, and the right to privacy.

The ICPD Programme of Action also identifies the empowerment of women as central to the achievement of reproductive health. "Advancing gender equality and equity and the empowerment of women, and the elimination of all kinds of violence against women, and ensuring women's ability to control their own fertility, are corner-stones of population and development programmes". Reproductive health as out-lined in the ICPD Programme of Action, and widely recognized thereafter, is a life-time concern for both women and men. It is not confined to women of childbearing age.

Adequate food and nutrition are essential from conception to adulthood for proper growth and physical development, to ensure optimal work capacity and normal reproductive performance, and also to ensure the adequacy of immune mechanisms and resistance to infections. The risk of mortality in children under five years of age is also increased considerably by severe undernutrition. Nutritional status of a person depends on food consumption and not solely the production and availability of food. Dietary energy supply measurements assume that available food is distributed and consumed in relation to requirements which is often not the case. protein energy malnutrition (PEM), generally referred to simply as malnutrition, is an imbalance between the supply of protein and energy, and the body's demand for them to ensure optimal growth and function. Inadequate intake of food or essential nutrients leads to undernutrition, resulting in deterioration of physical growth and health. On the other hand, excess intake of high energy food relative to the body's needs results in overweight and obesity.

For women, the effects of poverty combine with Other factors that undermine nutritional status, such as cultural norms regarding food taboos, and food allocation within the household which is often unfavourable to females. As a consequence, an estimated 20-45% of women of childbearing age in the developing world do not eat the WHO recommended 2250 calories a day. The additional biological demands on women due to menstruation, pregnancy and lactation further accentuate the situation, making nutritional deficiencies the most widespread and disabling health problem among women in developing countries. For example, stunting in women particularly when combined with early pregnancy and poor weight gain during pregnancy can lead to obstructed labour, with life-threatening consequences. Iron deficiency anaemia makes pregnancy and delivery high-risk and life threatening events for women.

A vicious cycle of undernourishment and ill-health is set in motion: poorly nourished mothers giving birth to low birth-weightbabies. Low-birth--weight babies have 3-4 times greater risk of dying from diarrhoeal diseases, acute respiratory infections, and if not immunized, measles. They are more likely to be malnourished at 1 year, and by around 5 years of age, low-birth-weight babies may have had more cyclic episodes of infection and malnutrition and may be severely stunted. This will be carried into adult life. Baby girls born with a low birth weight are, in addition, likely to go through childhood and adolescence with a disadvantage in terms of feeding and care, and grow up to be severely undernourished adult women in poor health.

Recognizing the magnitude of the problem of malnutrition worldwide, global goals were set following the World Summit for Children in 1990 and reaffirmed at the International Conference on Nutrition in 1992. These goals are to:

(1) reduce severe and moderate malnutrition among children under five years of age by half of the 1990 levels,

(2) increase the percentage of newborns having an adequate birth weight (2500 grams or more) to 90%,

(3) reduce to less than 10%, and possibly eliminate iodine deficiency disorders,

(4) eliminate vitamin A deficiency and its consequences including blindness, and

(5) reduce iron deficiency anaemia.

Nutritional problems of public health concern affecting

vulnerable groups in the South- East Asia Region pose serious challenges to national health systems. These conditions include protein-energy malnutrition, and deficiencies of micronutrients, such as iron, iodine and vitamin A.

In the last decade much work has been done on identifying the linkages between gender and the environment, the interaction between environmental factors and gender on women's health remains a relatively unexplored area. The present discussion remains illustrative rather than substantive, owing to the serious limitation of hard data – both qualitative and quantitative – that reveal the interaction between gender, health and environment. The important biological differences by sex which put women and men at differential risks from environmental factors have often been recognized when examining environmental health issues. When compared to men, women have a smaller stature, their vital capacity is 11% less, and their haemoglobin is approximately 20% less. They have a larger skin surface area when compared to circulating volume, and more fat content in their bodies. However, this constitutes only one part of a gendered understanding of environmental health issues. In almost all societies, women and men tend to occupy, use and manage aspects of the biophysical envi-ronment in a gender differentiated manner.

Women and men engage in different spheres of activity, and the amount of time they spend interacting with various elements of the environment tend to vary. It may therefore be anticipated that the nature and degree of the environmental health risks to which women and men are exposed would be different. Despite this, few studies have examined environmental risks and health consequences from such a perspective.

Environmental Health

Environmental health hazards include traditional hazards arising from human activity and natural phenomena, such as poor sanitation and contaminated drinking water, and indoor air pollution. They also include modern hazards, such as outdoor air pollution, water pollution from industrial effluents and the lowering of the water table, chemical and radiation hazards, and depletion of natural resources that have resulted from the pattern of economic development adopted by most countries.

Poor sanitation and contaminated drinking water are two of the most common environmental hazards in many countries of the world. Unsanitary excreta disposal and contamination of drinking water by pathogens are associated with diarrhoeal diseases which kill approximately three million children annually, and schisto-somiasis and intestinal helminth infection which affect hundreds of millions each year.

In fact the lack of adequate sanitation facilities and unsafe drinking water represents a serious health threat in countries of the South-East Asia Region, where in the majority of countries, 30-75% of the population are not covered by sanitation facilities. In crowded settlements and areas lacking adequate sewage facilities, contamination of ground and surface water sources used for drinking, washing and cleaning is very common.

Faecal contamination of drinking water and food is associated with hepatitis A, a common viral infection in all countries of the Region. Most countries are also highly endemic for hepatitis E, an infection with potentially fatal consequences to pregnant women. Data gathered by WHO show that more than 60 water-borne outbreaks of hepatitis E were reported from Bangladesh, India, Indonesia, Myanmar and Nepal during the last 20 years. Approximately four million cases of HEV infection occur in the Region every year. Although not having re-solved the "traditional" organic water pollution problems from poor quality water supply and lack of sanitation facilities, countries of the Region are, at the same time, faced with "modern" toxic pollution problems from organic matter contained in industrial effluents. Many rivers and water bodies are becoming saturated with organic compounds from industrial effluents, posing a major threat to both human health and aquatic life.

The rough construction of industries in areas with access to one of the major river systems, and direct dumping of untreated industrial effluents into Nepal's Bagmati and Bishnumati rivers, have resulted in high concentrations of sodium, potassium and chlorine. In Indonesia the results of about 20 studies on rivers have shown that even those used to supply drinking water are heavily polluted. Water from the lakes of Gunung Sewu in Yogyakarta previously used for household purposes and for drinking are now polluted and unfit for human consum-ption. This is also true of wells in the Jakarta area which have been found to be contaminated by detergents and nitrates, while shallow wells have significant levels of organic and coliform contamination. Pollution of water sources previously fit for human consumption adds to women's workload in fetching water from alternative sources.

Contamination

Arsenic contamination of ground water, the main source of drinking water, has been detected in 7 districts of West Bengal, India and in 23 districts of Bangladesh. Arsenic poisoning is slow and cumulative, and it takes several years for symptoms to appear. Symptoms include melanosis (abnormal black-brown pigmentation of the skin), hyperkeratosis (thickening) of the palms and soles, gangrene of the lower extremities, and skin cancer. In extreme cases of hyperkeratosis, the soles and palms of the patient are covered by black bulbous swellings. The disfigurements caused by arsenic poisoning often result in the social ostracisation of the persons affected, much like in the case of leprosy. The consequences to women are especially harsh, and several cases of desertion and divorce have been documented in a field report from one of the many affected districts.

Besides the air pollution is a serious environmental health hazard affecting the populations of developing and developed countries alike. Indoor air pollution is mainly associated with the use of biomass fuels for cooking in settings with poor ventilation. Industrial emissions and automobiles are the principle sources of outdoor air pollution. Suspended particulate matter (SPM) including lead, gaseous inorganic pollutants such as sulphur dioxide, carbon monoxide and nitrogen oxides, as well as hydrocarbons and volatile organic compounds are among some of the major air pollutants. All of these cause considerable damage to health. Suspended particulate matter contribute to respiratory problems, and this is especially true of SPM under 10 microns, which are so small that they penetrate deeply into the lung. SPM under 10 microns are also more closely linked to cancer, particularly if they are of hydrocarbon origin. Lead affects the circulatory, nervous and reproductive systems as well as the kidneys.

Carbon monoxide, if inhaled by pregnant women, may threaten the growth and mental development of the foetus. Nitrogen oxides increase susceptibility to viral infections, and can irritate the lungs and cause bronchitis and pneumonia. A few studies from the Region have shown that women's responsibility for cooking exposes them to this risk disproportionately more than men. Chronic bronchitis was the most common illness, followed by bronchial asthma, pulmonary tuberculosis and bronchiectasis (chronic dilation of one or more bronchi). Bronchial asthma and pulmonary tuberculosis were common in the younger age groups, while for women above the age of 40 years, 42% had chronic bronchitis and 27% had bronchiectasis.

In a hospital-based study shows that, the incidence over a 15-year period of cor pulmonale (right-sided heart failure due to disease of the lungs) was found to be similar for both sexes. However, while 75% of the men affected were smokers, only 10% of the women were. The age at onset of cor pulmonale was also 10-15 years earlier in women than in men. The study concluded that these illnesses among women were due to exposure to smoky fireplaces.A study in one urban and three rural areas in Nepal in 1988 recorded high prevalence rates of chronic bronchitis and cor pulmonale for both men and women. This was despite the fact that the women were very light smokers. Outdoor air pollution is escalating rapidly in all major cities, including those in the South-East Asia Region. The problem is especially acute in megacities, several of which are in this Region. According to a 1992 WHO/United Nations Environment Programme (UNEP) study, the SPM levels in five megacities in the Region exceeded the limits according to WHO guidelines by a factor of two.

Women Empowerment

Women Empowerment is a process which change existing power relations by addressing itself to the three dimensions material, human and intellectual resources. It is a process which must challenge and change ideology, the set of ideas, attitudes, beliefs and practices in which gender bias or social bias like caste, class, regionalism and communalism are embedded. The failure to address the ideology makes many empowerment programs ineffective in really changing gender relations in the long term. Empowerment processes must of cause also change power relations through redistribute resources, by giving people much more equal access and control over sources.

Since the ideology is embedded in institutions and structures it must work to transform these institutions and structures. If not the gender contract is rethought, particularly at the household level, the ideology will keep on influencing. Addressing transformation of ideological environment, in the way people think is a very integrate and critical task of the empowerment process. This task of changing the ideology is believed to be hard. However, it is not hard to do with women, as people who are oppressed always somehow know that they are oppressed, they only need a social environment which permits them to articulate the oppression. The processes of empowerment has to occur at several levels. The transformation has to give changes in the ideological system, in access to resources and in institutions and structures at several levels, such as the family and the household, the village and the community, the state and the market.

There has to be an extrinsic process where things in the outside environment are changed, by which is meant women's greater control over resources. But just as important and much more critical is the intrinsic process, the change of the ideological environment. There is a need to increase women's self-confidence. This make women gaining strength and motivation to sustain their empowerment.

The women's image of themselves understanding of their capacities have to change. Otherwise they are conditioned from birth to uphold male power, privilege and prestige. The change in the intrinsic level is critical in any process of empowerment. Empowerment is not only an external process, but a process that has to bring about these intrinsic changes, in women but in also in men. When women get organised and raise their consciousness about their disempowerment, and use their critical understanding to organise themselves and struggle for greater access to resources there are very few problems from the men. The problems come when the women challenge practices within the home and men's control over them.

Threat of Force

Force and violence or the threat of force and violence is deeply internalised in women in the South Asian society and is the outer boundary which perpetuates existing gender relations. Internal control is exercised by the women out of fear for that force if they go beyond certain boundaries. When women get organised and raise their consciousness about their disempowerment, and use their critical understanding to organise themselves and struggle for greater access to resources there are very few problems from the men. Internal control is exercised by the women out of fear for that force if they go beyond certain boundaries. Several institutions and structures in the society such as the family, the educational system, the religion and several others as well as the social, economic, legal and political structures constantly reproduce these power relations, because inherent in these institutions and structures is this ideology. The ideological element is embedded in the institutions and structures, therefore they reinforce the ideology and through this inequitable access and control over the resources. In most of the countries of South Asia it is impossible and unwise to address gender as a separate set of inequalities, without addressing caste and class. As class, caste and gender are interwoven in women's lives they need to be addressed at the same time. A common conception in South Asia is that the women are their own worst enemies. This myth can be broken through closer examine and understanding the social dynamics and the psycho dynamics of oppression.

By this the consent and participation of the oppressed in their discrimination is obtained. First through force, then through a whole set of social rules and structural barriers, and indoctrination. At the psychological level this operates in several ways. In the South Asian context women's status is gained from men. Women's power is restricted to the private domain, while men rule both the private and the public domain. Women's power is exercised through their influence on men, so therefore, women must become rivals and compete with each other for power. Thus, the oppressed uphold the oppressors power. They have often come in a situation of policing each other, and punishing their deviant members. The oppressors have been relieved of that minor task. The parents indoctrinate their children in the ideology of oppression and its social rules.

The problems of power dynamics and how adolescents experience power are to be explored in order to know how to deal with the situation in which many adolescents are today. The need to empower adolescents has not been acknowledged. The knowledge about adolescents is limited. In the western world there is a tendency to see adolescents relations in a romantic light and therefore deny the power struggles in these relationships. Some studies have shown that adolescents are experiencing violent dating relationships and sexual coercion. In the developing countries there has been a high raise of aids, and the rate of unintended pregnancies is high.

Several AIDS intervention strategies have recently begun to question those interventions who rely on that women can control the sexual encounter. It has been realised that women alone can not reinforce condom use without having active participation of men. The great age gap in marriages, which is common in developing countries, leads to a powerlessness for the adolescents. The international attention has only just begun to be paid to the economic bases of power. Adolescents are particularly vulnerable to this. It is socially accepted for old men to have sexual relations with young girls. The school girls often lack resources to go to school and they therefore enter such relations to be able to get an education. Families prefer to spend money on educating boys. Sex becomes a way for girls to get an education, especially on higher levels of education. There is a serious problem of male teachers demanding sex in return for good grades.

Labour Market

At the labour market it is not unusual with bosses expecting sex as condition for employment and promotion. The system of paying with sex can thus permeate the world of the adolescents. In South Asia there is a phenomena of bride wealth linked to education. In the region bride wealth is the exchange for marriage. Parents are now facing limited resources why they get prospective suitors to pay for the school fees for the girls. When the prospective suitors, who is supposed to be like their fiancees, pay the school fees they use that as bride wealth, and the men want to see some in return for their money. So the family push their girls into sexual relations with these men even while they are in school. If a pregnancy occurs they just take them from school and send them to live with their husband. This bride wealth is so tied up with female education, particularly among poorer families, so if girls want to get secondary education they often have very restricted choice. When talking about how adolescents experience power it is important to also look beyond access to resources and look at culturally defined social relations.

Parental power can for instance mean that parents arrange marriages, denies adolescents contraception, decides whether an unmarried pregnant woman should have an abortion or not, or prevents the adolescents to seek the health care that they need. In many countries there are multiple systems of justice. There is a legal minimum age of marriage, but it only applies to the 25 per cent who are thought to be governed by statutory law. For those who are governed by customary law the parents can arrange marriage at any time, there is no minimum age.

Land and Cattle

Women do usually not have access to resources, such as land and cattle, unless being married. Therefore marriage is very important to the women. It is also important that the wife gets children to solidify their positions and try to make sure to get access to resources through children as there is no from each other. If women are not educated and the government does not have positive discrimination in terms of children's education, insisting that parents send their daughters to school, and penalising parents that do not send their daughters to school, female adolescents inaccessibility to resources will continue. Those girls value marriage and child-bearing as a way to access resources, because those are their options.

Most cultures have defined what it means to be masculine and feminine. To be feminine often means to be non aggressive, non assertive, to listen to the husband and parents, whereas masculinity means to be assertive. A number of studies show that male adolescent subscribe to masculine ideology which means that they should be assertive and not listen to what the women say, as they have been raised like that. These male adolescents are the ones who will have more sexual partners in a relationship, they will have less consistent condom use, they have less belief that males have responsibility to prevent pregnancy, and they believe that if the women gets pregnant that defines and validates their masculinity.

The gender role socialisation means for the females that they should be submissive to the males, the females shall be subordinate in a sexual relation. That impacts of course on whether they can say no to unwanted sex, use contraception, or even just talk to their partners about how to protect themselves from HIV and sexually transmitted diseases. Another important issue is sexual aggression and sexual coercion. It is common that females are coerced into sexual relationships.

To empower adolescents it is important to let them know how power operates in their lives. They also have to recognise how they as individuals and how the communities are affected by the way power operates. Many people do not recognise that they are powerless, because you tend to think that "this is the way society works, and has done for generations". The adolescents also develop skills of how to change the power balances in society. Most important is to make them psychologically believe that they can control their own lives. Peer counselling is an important way of spreading the empowerment. Empowerment at group level can be very efficient. When an adolescent gains power over her own life and has understood that all the adolescents are subjected to certain conditions she can help others in getting power over their lives. It is also important to understand the female socialisation process and the gender role stereotyping.

From a demographic point of view it is important to get the adolescents able to exercise their reproductive choices. This can mean to chose not to engage in sexual activity, not to engage in sexual activity without informed consent, to get males to conform to safe sexual practices, to ensure not being at risk for unintended pregnancy or a sexually transmitted disease, ability to negotiate pleasurable sex. It is important not to only focus on the married adolescents but also on the unmarried who have a more vulnerable economic situation and who also have a greater risk of getting sexually exploited.

If girls are to be empowered their access to resources such as basic education has to increase. However, in schools the gender stereotypes are still strong and gender socialisation is enforced in schools. If girls are given access to resources independent of the family, their capacity to achieve a favourable balance of power in relationships can be enhanced. Their independence from the families, who often have very strong influence on adolescent girls, can be increased. Wider social networks could be developed and create less dependence of men and children. Without access to resources the women have to depend of men and children for survival and also for status. Access to information and services can foster feelings of empowerment and has to be increased. Many adolescents have a poor knowledge about safe sex, and distorted ideas and faulty knowledge of how likely they are to get pregnant. Information would empower them to know how to protect them selves towards unwanted pregnancies.

Situation of Women

Education is an important indicator of women's empowerment. Even though women are the majority of the students and graduates and a large number of women are employed in education, not many women make careers or get top positions in the field of education or research. The girls have less opportunities to attend high schools that prepare them for professions as some of the schools that traditionally has accommodated them have been closed up, such as tailoring schools due to the crisis of the textile industry. At the same time some of the technical schools do not accept girls. Altogether this leads to fewer opportunities of a vocational training for the girls. When the costs for the education are rising it has been observed that families tend to prefer to invest in the boys education rather than the girls. One of the issues that would need to be addressed is the perpetuation of gender stereotypes in the educational systems. The schoolbooks and manuals still mediate gender stereotypes, the women are mostly portrayed as house bound whilst the men have attractive professions. Stereotypes acquired in the youth will be hard to remove, why these stereotypes contribute to strengthen the patriarchy.

Women's situation on the labour market has deteriorated as they have shown to be less successful than men to compete for jobs in market environment. Women are easier fired and have more difficulties in finding jobs. The proportion of unemployed women are increasing, and the number of unrecorded cases is larger among the women. The phenomenon of sectoral segregation is a fact. Women's employment is concentrated into feminised jobs in the service sector and in light industries such as the textile industry, food processing, supply services, education, health etc. These sectors are wage discriminated. The wage gap between men and women is persistent. The discrimination against women takes place in two ways; employed women are paid less than their male counterparts if they do the same job; the sectors that has a high proportion of women tend to be less paid.

While most people, perhaps, imagine that nearly all women marry and are supported by their husbands, those who know better how women live, or die, have rarely anything to say on the subject. Such social problems as this are certainly painful; they may or may not be insoluble; they must not be ignored. The phrase "to become a governess" is sometimes used as if it were a satisfactory outlet for any unsupported woman above the rank of housemaid. The facts of the society have changed more rapidly than its conventions. Formerly muscles did the business of the world, and the weak were protected by the strong; now brains do the business of the world, and the weak are protected by law. The industrial disabilities of women, unavoidable under the earlier regime, have become cruel under the later.

The desire for education which is widely felt by South Asian women, and which has begun to find its expression in many practical ways, is a desire which springs from no conceit of cleverness, from no ambition of the prizes of intellectual success, as is sometimes falsely imagined, but from the conviction that for many women to get knowledge is the only way to get bread, and still more from that instinctive craving for light which in many is stronger than the craving for bread.

Any effort in the cause of governesses is important, not only as it affects individuals at this moment engaged in the profession, but still more in its bearing upon the future of all

South Asian girls and women, through the prospect which it holds out of an improved education for the daughters of the middle classes, who, more and more, will have to maintain themselves. And if we think how much honour and dignity ought to attach to the office of a teacher we should, from the highest motives be anxious to raise the character and social standing of those who seek that office. The old social order has changed, giving place to the new, but women have fallen out of line with the onward movement, fettered by their own cowardice and the careless selfishness of men. Custom and use press heavily on women, they endure long before they dare to think whether the system under which they suffer is a right or a wrong one, whether their burdens be removable or no,— whether, in short, they have fallen into the hands of man. Even when they are fully persuaded that their burdens are removable, they have no voice to raise. Exclusion of women from trades is in most cases notoriously based upon a coarse selfishness. Take the instance of the china painters at Worcester. It appears that both men and women are employed in this art, but that the women having excited the jealousy of the men by surpassing them in skilful execution, and consequently earning better wages, were by them forcibly deprived of the maulsticks on which it is necessary to rest the wrist while painting.

Thus the women are at once rendered incapable of any fine work, and can only be employed in the coarser kinds of paining. The masters submit to this tyranny, though to their own disadvantage, being probably afraid of a strike or riot if they resist, and the women are forced to yield from the fear of personal violence from their less skilful but heavier-fisted rivals.

The justice of educated men could scarcely be brought to bear upon a subject where chivalry and justice are needed more. In this matter, of the bad effects of trades' unions, much may be hoped for from the known character of working men themselves as a class. They are not wanting in justice, in tenderness of heart, and in a shrewd perception of right and wrong when they are placed before them: but they need enlightenment and instruction, from those who are their superiors in education and trained intelligence. Untold good might be done, and much future misery averted, if those among our leading men who have the ear and the confidence of working-men would bring before them fairly and patiently, such subjects as these.

Economics lie at the very root of practical morality, and it is to be hoped that men of influence, and genius, and experience of life, will address themselves gravely to the task of instructing the working classes on this most grave subject. The common objection brought before the society for promoting the employment of women, is that a risk would be incurred of decreasing the employment of men. Now, in the first place, this is by no means certain. No one proposes to interfere with the men at present working at any trade; but while the demand for young men at high wages in the colonies continues practically unlimited, it may be questioned whether the admission to a sedentary employment at home is not a pitfall as often as an advantage.

Many a young man would be healthier and happier at some manly trade in Canada or Australia, than in standing behind an English counter or plaiting straw. To take only the trades connected with women's dress and such matters, the census gives the following numbers of men employed in trades, some of which would seem as distinctly appropriate to the one sex, as soldiering and sailoring to the other. Defective training of the women themselves is the most serious of all the hindrances. Here the vicious circle returns upon itself. These women cannot teach, because they are so ill educated.

Several rejected from the shop-till or housekeeper's room for ignorance and inefficiency, is compelled to offer herself among the lowest class of nursery governesses, or, failing all, to embrace the career, the avenues to which stand ever wide open, yawning like the gates of hell, when all other doors are closed. The fault of this defective training lies mainly with the middle-class parents who educate their daughters to get husbands, and for nothing else. Education was what the slave-owners most dreaded for their slaves, for they knew it to be the sure road to emancipation.

Undoubtedly there are many who are quickly weary of any though which is perplexing or painful: nevertheless the facts remain the same—that women constitute one half of the human race, that whatever effects them, for good or evil, affects not one half, but the whole of the human race, and that the primary education of all generations of men rests in the hands of women.

There are two classes of advocates of the improvement of the education and condition of women. The one class urge everything from the domestic point of view. They argue in favour of all which is likely to make women better mothers, or better companions for men, but they seem incapable of judging of a woman as a human being by herself, and superstitiously afraid of anything which might strengthen her to stand alone, prepared, single-handed, to serve her God and her country. When it is urged upon them that the women who do and must stand alone are counted by millions, they are perplexed, but only fall back on expressions of a fear lest a masculine race of women should be produced, if we admit any theories respecting them apart from conjugal and maternal relationships. The other class who speak with some slight contempt of maternity, in whose advocacy there appears little evidence of depth of thought, or tenderness, or wisdom, and which bespeaks a dry, hard, unimaginative conception of human life. They appear to have no higher ideal for a woman than that of a man who has been "tripos'ed," and is going to "get on in the world," either in the way of making money or acquiring fame. They speak of women as if it were a compliment to them, or in any way true, to say that they are like men.

The first class of advocates do not know how strong nature is, how true she is for the most part, and how deeply the maternal character is rooted in almost all women, married or unmarried: they are not, therefore, likely to see that when a better education is secured to women, when permission is granted them not only to win bread for themselves, but to use for the good of society, we may expect to find that they will become the more and not the less womanly. Every good quality, very virtue which we regard as distinctively feminine, will, under conditions of greater freedom, develop more freely, like plants brought out into the light from a cellar in which they languished, dwarfed and blanched, without sun or air. The woman is strong in almost every woman; and it may be called an infidelity against the truth of nature to suppose that the removal of unjust restrictions, and room given to breathe freely, and to do her work in life without depression and without bitterness, will cause her to cast off her nature. It will always be in her nature to foster, to cherish, to take the part of the weak, to train, to guide, to have a care for individuals, to discern the small seeds of a great future, to warm and cherish those seeds into fullness of life. The second kind of advocacy of the rights of women, may be said to be simply a reaction against the first. It is chiefly held by a few women of superior intellect who feel keenly the disadvantages of their class, their feebleness, through want of education, against public opinion, which is taken advantage of by base people, their inability, through want of representation, to defend their weaker members, and the dwarfing of the faculties of the ablest and best among them.

These women have associated little with men, or at best, know very little of their inner life, and do not therefore see as clearly as they see their own loss, the equal loss that it is to men, and the injury it involves to their characters, to live dissociated from women : they therefore look forth from their isolation with something of an excusable envy on the freer and happier lot, which includes, they believe, a greater power to do good, and imagine that the only hope for themselves is to push into the ranks of men, to demand the same education, the same opportunities, in order that they may compete with them on their own ground. They have lost the conception of the noblest development possible for both men and women; for assuredly that which men, for the most part, aim at, is not the noblest, and yet that is what such women appear to which to imitate; they have lost sight of the truth, too, that men and women were made equal indeed, but not alike, and were meant to supplement one another, and that in so doing,—each supplying force which the other lacks,—they are attracted with a far greater amount of impulse to a common centre.

Anyone who will candidly and carefully consider the histories of separate communities of men or women, for educational or other purposes, must see that the evils attendant on such a system as they represent outweigh its conveniences. The arrangement is for a given period, but not so the evils which accompany it, for they,—and of this men are not ignorant,—too often leave their effects throughout life. The objection rises at once of the difficulty of adopting any other arrangement than the present, which may be called an unnatural one. This objection will be more effectually met by facts than by reasoning, and in time facts will speak for themselves, while up to the present they attest that whenever the experiment of a different system has been tried, the difficulties have been found to be very much less than it was believed they would be, before the trial was made.

Women in Politics

The process of building new democratic systems and market economies continues without women's participation and without consultation with them on their concerns and priorities. In the field of political participation it is easy to observe that the women have lost in the nineties. To get a deeper understanding of the political participation of women during the communist era there is a need to look beyond these absolute figures. When closer examining the past a different picture emerge. Few of the women who were engaged in politics before the transformation reached higher positions or the inner circle and therefore their impact on the politics not was so big. Now, even though there are less women participating in the politics their opportunity to really influence decision making and look after the women's interests in the new democratic system are greater.

Participation of women in national committees and bodies is limited to "soft" committees dealing with social issues rather than those with lager resources such as budget and finance committees. Female participation in executive power has been extremely low. There are very few female ministers or women having higher posts in the civil services. There is an inherited structure from the former regime where the women are not represented in positions of economic power. This can not be attributed to their education as many women are educated in the field of economy.

Women's Health

The women's reproductive health is not a priority issue for the decision makers in the region. It is neither perceived as a priority issue of international donors as the region does not experience over population. The problems are therefore often overlooked. The Eastern Europe has decreasing fertility rates, which revitalises ideologies which threaten the countries with slogans of the extinction of the nation, if women do not have more children. These ideologies are often based on religious or nationalistic values that promote "family values", which in general view a woman in traditional roles of mother of many children and a house wife. These tendencies have contributed to establish strong anti-abortion movements. Abortion was generally legalised much earlier in the region than in the developed countries, and it was widely used because family planning was not prevalent. Some of the countries in the region have now tried to restrict the liberal abortions laws or at least limiting the access to abortion services.

Campaigning against contraception is increasing, the arguments are mainly religious, but also quasi-medical. The problem of sexually transmitted diseases is increasing in the region. These problems are not recognised by the governments who try to deny the seriousness of the problem. Lack of sex education increase the dangers of spreading HIV infections. Due to this the problem of HIV can soon grow severely. The sex industry is continuously growing and the problems it entails is affecting many women's lives. The problems have now been recognised by the UN. The new phenomena of trafficking in women from east to west has reached an epidemic size, and the growth of extremely young victims is big.

Violence against women is a serious problem in the region and legal regulations does not exist. A concrete problem is that there is not sufficient shelters for victims. Some small groups have now started to work with these questions, but there is still a long way to go concerning these matters. Although the process of democratic and economic changes was expected and welcomed for so long by most societies of South Asia, it has also brought some negative side-effects, particularly for women. These side-effects make women not equally benefiting from the changes and opportunities in the new democratic market economies. The lack of sufficient consciousness among women about equality issues contributes to the deteriorating situation of women. The women's organisations of the region are very few, they are now starting to develop, but they are yet not strong enough to articulate the demand for equality. There is still an absence of a legal framework of equality in the region. Small signs of a change can now be seen, Poland is presently making an attempt to make a legislation similar to the one of Sweden to promote women. The democracy will be the real starting point for the women of South Asia to mobilise and raise their consciousness for the future.

Mobilising and organising is important as it is nearly impossible for individual women to break out of the gender system in the context of South Asia. When groups of women do this process together they reinforce each other and the strength of the collective has a great role. The collective then becomes an alternative, a non traditional environment, where women can think dangerous thoughts and have revolutionary ideas, and the activists working with the women can give them access to information, knowledge and skills. They then go through a process of identifying their own priorities and the strategies they want to use to struggle for change, whether it is to struggle for resources or for changes in gender relations in the home. They act and they analyse the action, what worked and what did not work. This is a spiral where your raise your consciousness to a new level and then you continue to new actions, new struggles and so on.

The process of women empowerment has to be one which addresses all sources and structures of power. It is not enough to give women education, access to the labour market and employment. It will not transform gender and caste relations. The process has to work on both an individual and a collective level. Women have to be organised and they have to be acknowledged as a political force. The process has to challenge both gender and social power relations. It is a process that is much about education, but education defined in a different way. It does not come out of a school book, knowledge has to be expanded. More importantly it has to enable people to think critically and to question. It has to generate new notions about power itself. Otherwise when women enter the public structures, given the existing ideology, they operate with the so called male notions of power which is power as domination, patronage etc.

An empowerment process which simply facilitates women to gain access to forms of political power and structures that exist today would be very counter productive. The process also has to enable women to challenge and change the meaning of power in itself. The process is very multi layered and multi pronged.

The women's empowerment will lead to both disadvantages and advantages for men. In the context of South Asia the empowerment of women can to an extent lead to the disempowerment of men. The redistribution of rights and responsibility within households, in the communities and in the states mean that men have to give up what have been their traditional privileges. Men will lose their traditional control over women's labour, income, sexuality, reproduction and mobility. There will have to be a change in the gender based division of labour. Not just in sharing housework and child care, but also in the work places where gender divisions are still rigid. The violence against women has to stop and the protection of women against violence must increase. Men will not have any greater rights to, or control over, children, household assets and resources, and no greater inheritance rights than have women. The empowerment of women will also lead to gains for men. Men are in some ways also oppressed by gender systems. Gender stereotypes disables men from being whole persons. If men are free of gender stereotyping and can express or discover so called "feminine" sides of themselves they will get happier. Women will be equal partners, and able to share "male" work and responsibilities. The men will be free psychologically of the "oppressor" role, which might have very serious implications for them.

States have a general enabling role in the process of women's empowerment. Donors could support states in taking these steps. States have to remove structural barriers and biases in their own policies and programmes. They have to create spaces for women in the design, implementation and monitoring of programs and policies. They have to reform the legal systems and the judicial systems to remove the inequalities that are enshrined and embedded in law. Equal access for women to public resources and services provided by the state has to be ensured. The most important role of the states is to implement and enforce the agreements and the protection of women's rights.

A complete empowerment process which has a greater chance not only to succeed in the short term but to bring about long term and sustainable changes is a synergetic process where the state contribute through creating conditions. The state can not, and should not, empower women. What the state can do is to create enabling conditions which legitimise a change in women's position. Grass roots and community processes are also needed, the civil society's organisations, women's organisations and NGOs has a role to play. The actors of civil society should contribute in organising women, building public awareness, training and gender sensitisation, providing services to unreached, public policy watching, market watching, public information, monitoring violations, public information, autonomous research, innovations and experimentation, advocacy and advisory work.

For millions of activists in the global women's movement, - twenty years after the launching of the Women Decade, ten years after Nairobi - The Beijing Declaration on Gender and Equality has become a metaphor for transformation. The United Nations Fourth World Conference was the largest mobilisation of the global women's movement to date. Nearly every country of the world and tens of thousands of people participated in the multi-year process that culminated in Beijing in September 1995.

Over 40,000 women made it to China to participate in the NGO Forum to cover the conference for the media and to negotiate and agree upon the Platform for Action with its 12 spheres of preoccupation: Poverty, education, health, violence, armed conflict, economy, participation in political decision making, institutional mechanisms, human rights, media, environment and the girl. Holding governments and international agencies to their promises of social commitments is a challenge that must be met in today's climate of impoverishing globalisation. In fact, never has there been a greater consensus on human development at a time when conditions are so unconducive for it. Unsustainable production and consumption patterns, from economic globalisation and growth that is, in the words of the UNDP's Human Development Report 1996, "rootless, ruthless, jobless, voiceless and futureless". Whatever the debating points, there can scarcely be any doubt that the Beijing Platform is a unifying force propelling change in the lives of millions of women today as perhaps never before. After Beijing, there have been a virtual explosion of feminist mobilisation.

Much of the initial responses to the Beijing platform have been in creating new mechanisms, upgrading existing structures and energising participatory processes. Concrete action plans or budgetary allocation are not the norm. Many recognise the goodwill gestures some governments have made to disseminate the results of Beijing in local languages, to consult with NGOs and to include activists in the agenda-setting for national action plans and follow-up mechanisms.

Many Latin American countries report the formation of commissions, interministerial and/or with NGO representation, to follow UP on agreements. Peru created a commission for women in Congress, the first such since independence. In South Africa, the office on the status of women is being established within the presidency. Other African nations are less ambitious, settling for gender focal points in ministries, as in Zimbabwe.

Interministerial commissions are also emerging in some countries, such as Russia, Austria and Bangladesh. A heartening feature of committees formed in some parts of Asia and Latin America is the governments' willingness to involve NGOs as consulting partners for the first time, both during the Beijing Process and after. This is seen as an especially important breakthrough in Pakistan, where the bureaucracy has no tradition of working with members or groups from civil society.

Women in some countries have wrested key victories in the equally contested terrain of domestic violence. In Colombia and Malaysia a bill to eradicate violence in the family became law and in Nicaragua a proposal has been submitted to the Congress. Costa Rica has launched a national plan for the detection of family violence.

Reforms on the law are also on the cards in Peru. Egypt

has recently banned the practice of female genital mutilation despite strong cultural opposition. Denmark has targeted for special attention the practice of female genital mutilation in its plans to mainstream a gender perspective in international cooperation.

With concerted actions by NGOs and UN agencies, governments report some encouraging initiatives to tackle the difficult problem of sexual exploitation, Particularly of girls, A World Congress Against Commercial Sexual Exploitation of Children, was convened by Sweden, UNICEF and BCPAT in August to agree upon a specific Plan of action to halt trafficking, prostitution and pornography involving girls and boys 18 years old and under. Japan has continued its process of Public apology to women and Payment of reparations to women known and "comfort women" who where sexually victimised during World War II, although activists insist that Public funds should be used, not private moneys, to convey the public weight of responsibility for these human rights violations. While laws alone cannot safeguard women, the enactment of penal and civil sanctions in domestic legislation forms and integral part of the Platforms strategic objectives in dealing with violence against women.

Future of Women

Young people normally go to school, and they love watching Indian movies. There is also paramilitary training for youngsters. Tourism also has had its influence despite of the effort to isolate tourists on resorts without any native population. Short pants and sleeveless shirts were not allowed in Male' in the early years of tourism but already in 1988 one could see very scant clothes on many tourists, who were no more harassed by the police. Alcohol rules for tourists are more relaxed, as well, but for a Maldivian sipping beer could still cause criminal penalties.

Officially the sexual relations are strictly controlled - sex is only allowed within marriage - but in practice there also seems to be lax behaviour. A young man who was suspected to have pre-marital relations with scout-girls was placed under house-arrest for several months. Banishment to remote islands and house-arrest are typical traditional punishments.

The Maldive Islands have been an independent state since early in the Christian era. The earliest mention is perhaps by Ammianus Marcellinus, who wrote that in 362 the Roman Emperor Julian received embassies *ab usque Divis et Serendivis*. The Serendivi are clearly from Sri Lanka (Seren= Ceylon), the Divi may be from the Maldives, whose name to its own inhabitants is *Divehi Rajje*, 'the island kingdom'. In the ninth century Sulaiman the merchant describes them as ruled by a queen. The people were probably already Buddhists, as is shown by remains of stupas on various islands, and it seems that the power of the sovereign extended over the whole 500 miles of the group from Minicoy in the north to Addu in the south, and that Male (which is central) was already the capital. Maldivians have always depended on trade for supplies of grain and textiles, which are not available on the islands, in return for fish, coconut products, ambergris and cowries; these last were used, in huge quantities, as international currency. Recent excavations in Male testify to regular visits of Chinese traders on their west-bound journeys by the tenth century. In 1153, the Maldive king was converted to Islam, either by Yusuf Shams ud Din of Tabriz or by Abul Barakat the 'Berber', and from this time onwards there is a written history of sultanate, compiled in Arabic, originally in 1725, supplemented by a few records in Divehi (Maldivian), a language akin to Sinhala.

A lengthy description of the islands is given by the North African traveller Ibn Battuta, who resided there for two separate periods in 1343-44 (when he became Qazi or Chief Justice) and 1346. Though the islands were solidly Muslim by this time, they still happened to be ruled by a queen, and Ibn Battuta commented unfavourably on the latitude allowed to women there.

The Portuguese became involved in Maldivian affairs during their struggle with Mamale of Kannanur in southwest India, who claimed suzerainty over the king of the Maldives, and they occupied Male from 1558 to 1573, after the then king had become a Christian. They were expelled by the efforts of Bodu Muhammad Takurufanu, founder of a new dynasty and the greatest hero of Maldivian history, whose birthplace in a small northern island is kept as a shrine today. The northernmost island of Maliku (Minicoy) remained permanently under the control of Kannanur after this time.

In 1602 the Frenchman Francois Pyrard of Laval was ship-wrecked on one of the Maldivian islands, whence he was transported to Male and kept prisoner for five years. He learnt to speak the

Divehi language, and his account of the islands, published in France in 1611, after he had managed to escape, constitutes the most extensive description of the country available before the nineteenth century.

After 1645 the Maldivian government sent an annual embassy to the Dutch Governor in Ceylon, and to his successors the British Governors until 1947, but there was never a colonial occupation. A full survey of the islands was made in 1835 by Lts Young and Christopher of the Indian Navy, and in 1887 a British protectorate over the Maldives was declared. A British man-of-war paid an annual visit thereafter, but the islands were unhealthy and generally avoided, except for the Cambridge scientific expedition of 1899-1900 and the American expedition of 1901.

The Maldive kings in the latter part of the nineteenth century fell heavily into debt to resident Borah merchants from Gujarat, and the resulting intrigues in Male led the British government to some reluctant involvement in Maldivian politics in the early twentieth century. In 1932 the king (the title 'Sultan' was only used in formal contexts) was compelled by his nobles to accept a constitution; he was later deposed and exiled.

During World War II British forces used bases in Maldivian territory. Nationalization process has helped to restore a sense of pride but it has also intensified ethnic tensions and made the resolution of ethnic problems more difficult to achieve.

Rulers of the Maldives to the Mid-twentieth Century

1573-1584	Bodu Muhammad Takurufanu al Alam
1584-1609	Ibrahim ibn Muhammad
1609-1620	Husain Famuderi
1620-1648	Imad ud Din Muhammad I
1648-1687	Ibrahim Iskandar I
1687-1691	Muhammad Ibn Ibrahim
1691-1692	Muhi ud Din Muhammad
1692	Shams ud Din Muhammad al Hamawi
1692-1700	Muhammad Ibn Hajji Ali
1700-1701	Ali
1701	Hasan ibn Ali
1701-1705	Muzhir ud Din Ibrahim
1705-1721	Imad Ud Din Muhammad II
1721-1750	Ibrahim Iskandar II
1750-1754	Imad ud Din Muhammad Mukarram

—	—
1760-1766	Izz ud Din Hasan Ghazi
1766-1773	Ghiyas ud Din Muhammad
1773-1774	Ghams ud Din Muhammad
1774-1778	Muizz ud Din Muhammad
1778-1798	Nur ud Din Muhammad
1798-1834	Muin ud Din Muhammad
1834-1882	Imad ud Din Muhammad III
1882-1886	Nur ud Din Ibrahim (first reign)
1886-1888	Muin ud Din Muhammad II
1888-1892	Nur ud Din Ibrahim (second reign)
1892-1893	Imad ud Din Muhammad IV
1893	Shams ud Din Muhammad Iskanda (first reign)
1893-1903	Imad ud Din Muhammad V
1903-1935	Shams ud Din Muhammad Iskandar (second reign)
1935-1945	Nur ud Din Hasan Iskandar
1945-1952	Abdul Majid Didi

Source : *R. F. Tapsell Monarchs Rulers Dynasties and Kingdoms of the World*, p. 445 (London, 1983).

After World War II, Muhammad Amin Didi took charge of the country (which was still nominally a monarchy, but with a Regency Committee instead of a monarch) and introduced numerous reforms. In January 1953 he changed the country from a monarchy to a Republic, with himself as first President; but his absences abroad allowed his opponents to overthrow him in September of the same year, and when he tried to return on December 31, 1953 he was attacked and injured in the streets and subsequently died. A nominal monarch was then restored who reigned until 1968, but without power. The government was at first under the control of Ibrahim Ali Didi, with whom the British government came to an agreement to reactivate a waritime base on Gan island in Addu Atoll. The economic and social influences exercised indirectly by the British forces paved the way for a breakaway movement (the 'Suvadive Republic') in the southern atolls, headed by Afif Didi, which was eventually put down but led to a bad relations with the British under Ibrahim Ali Didi's successor, Ibrahim Nasir. In 1965, complete severance from Britain was declared, and in 1968 the last king resigned and a second republic was instituted. Gan remained on lease, but the British government gave this up unilaterally in 1976. Nasir was replaced as President in 1979 by Maumun Abdul Gayum, and in 1982 the Maldives rejoined the Commonwealth.

Under Nasir's rule the modernization of the Maldives, begun by Amin Didi, was speeded up, particularly in Male. The Borahs and the Sri Lankan Moors were expelled, and foreign trade became a government monopoly. A merchant navy was acquired, trading largely with India and the Middle East. The two Government schools in Male (for boys and for girls) were converted into English-medium schools on the Sri Lankan pattern, with teaching staff brought over from Sri Lanka, and young Maldivians were sent abroad on training courses. The old aristocratic order of society in Male was thus greatly modified.

In 1972 the government of Sri Lanka suddenly discontinued their bulk purchases of dried fish from the Maldives. This had been the principal Maldivian export for over a century, and was channelled entirely through Sri Lanka, where it formed an essential curry-stuff. One result of this ban was the leasing out of fish-processing rights to a Japanese company, which stationed 'collecting vessels' at various points in the archipelago and purchased fish from Maldivian fishermen at agreed prices. Another was to give a sudden fillip to the development of tourism, involving regular air communications with the outside world and the introduction of such tourist essentials as alcohol (not available to Maldivians). The unexpected closure of the British post on Gan led to a large influx of Addu people into Male, and the population of the capital rose from 11,000 in 1967 to an estimated 35,000 in 1987. In order to accommodate these, it has been necessary to drain large areas of shallow lagoon. The past two decades has seen the internal affairs of this republic of atolls increasingly exposed to external forces.

Rulers of the Maldives since c. 1950

Head of State

Sultan

1945-1953 Amir Abdul Majid Didi

President

1953-1954 Amir Muhammad Amin Didi

Sultan

1954-1968 Amir Muhammad Farid Didi

President

1968-1978	Ibrahim Nasir
1978-	Maumun Abdul Gayum

Prime Minister (or equivalent post)

1945-1954	Amir Muhammad Amin Didi
1954-1957	Ibrahim Ali Didi
1957-1973	Ibrahim Nasir
1973-1975	Ahamed Zaki
1975-1978	Ibrahim Nasir
1978-	Maumun Abdul Gayum

Source : The Statesman's Yearbook 1950-1986/87.

2

Education and Employment

In Maldives, there is no institutional discrimination along gender lines in access to education and health services and for jobs in the public sector. School enrollment rates for girls and boys are almost the same. Women are employed in the pubic sector and in manufacturing, and they account for 70 percent of active persons in agriculture.

Nonetheless, women's access to higher education, necessary to respond to the new employment opportunities, is limited especially in the outer islands. In recent years, the Government, with ADB assistance, has been promoting increasing access to postsecondary education services to the population in the outer islands and women are expected to benefit significantly from such assistance.

The Government has taken further initiatives to support women in development, and a recent example includes the establishment by the Government of a Rf1 million micro credit scheme in March 2000, specifically for employment generation for women in the outer atolls.

Modernization efforts however, have helped make Maldives more homogeneous in the early 1990s. Traditionally, a significant gap has existed between the elite living on Male and the remainder of the population inhabiting the outer islands, these atolls distant from Male. Male, the traditional seat of the sultans and the nobility remains an elite society wielding political and economic power. Members of the several traditionally privileged ruling families; government, business, and religious leaders; professional; and scholars are found there. Male differs from other island communities also because as many as 40% of its residents are migrants. The island communities outside.

Islanders are in many instances interrelated by marriage and form a small, tightly knit group whose main economic pursuit is fishing. The family is the basic unit of society. Roughly 80% of Maldivian household consist of a single nuclear family composed of a married couple and their children rather than extended family. The man is usually the head of the family household, and descent is patrilineal. Women do not accept their husband names after marriage but maintain their maiden names. Inheritance of property is through both males and females. Traditional concepts concerning the way economies operate offer little well defined guidance when it comes to promoting women's empowerment or finding solutions towards a better economic justice between the sexes.

Women have to defend their right to paid work in the face of familial and community opposition, their right to better working conditions in the face of global competitive pressures, and their right to a better sharing out of and to an adequate support for unpaid care giving in the face of economic appraisals that do not take into account the costs and benefits of this type of work. Fishing, small-scale agriculture and tourism provide employment for over one-half of the workforce.

Tourism accounts for over one-quarter of government revenues and roughly 40% of foreign exchange receipts. Manufacturing accounts for 6% of gross domestic product. In 1995, the adult economic activity rate is less for women than men which is 28% for women and 74% for men, excluding armed forces. In 1998, the female labor force accounted for 43% of the total labor force. Women constitute 38% of government employees. While the Government does not expressly prohibit unions, it recognizes neither the right to form them. There were no reports of efforts to form unions during the year 2000. However, small groups of similarly employed workers with mutual interests have formed associations, which include employers as well as employees.

These associations may address a variety of issues, including worker's rights. There is no national minimum wage for the private sector, although the Government has established wage floors for certain kinds of work. Given the severe shortage of labor, employers must offer competitive pay and conditions to attract skilled workers.

Women who work for wages receive pay equal of men in the same positions. In the public sector, a 7-hours day and a 5-day workweek have been established through administrative circulars from the President's office. Overtime pay in the public sector was instituted in 1990. Employees are authorized 20 days of annual leaves, 30 days of medical leave, maternity leave of 60 days, and special annual leave of 10 days for extraordinary circumstances.

In 2000, in Maldives, based on the estimated population, there were 106 men for each 100 women. The projected life expectancy for women was 69 years, while it was 67 for men, a difference of 2 years. For each 1,000 individuals, the birth rate was 29 and the death rate was 5. The Government has built 10 of 15 planned women's centers in the atolls, which are facilities where family health workers can provide medical services. The centers also provide libraries and space for meetings and other activities with a focus of the development of women.

The percentage of deliveries attended by skilled health personnel in 1995/1998 is 90%. The maternal mortality rate is 350 per 100,000 live births for 1990/1998. A woman will have an average of 4.3 children in her life.

Out of 1,000 live children, the approximate number of infants who die within one year of birth (infant mortality rate) is higher for girls than boys, with a rate of 58 for girls and 43 for boys. The average rate of vaccination for main vaccines is 97,5%, and routine vaccination is covered by the government at 30%. The Government established a National Council for the Protection of the Child in 1992.

Government Policy

Government policy provides for equal access to educational and health programs for both male and female children. Laws protecting children's rights apply with equal force to children of either sex.

A 1992 law bars children under 14 of age from "places of waged work and from work that is not suitable for that child's age, health, or physical ability or that might obstruct the education or adversely affect the mentality or behavior of the child". An earlier law prohibits government employment of children under the age of 16.The Government does not prohibit specifically forced and bonded labor by children, but such practices are not known to occur.

Education is essential to the improvement of women's living standards and to allow them to take a more active part in the decision-making process within the family, the community, the place of paid work and the political arena. Basic literacy skills and other abilities are absolutely vital to the empowerment of women: without the skills acquired in secondary school, women cannot obtain better paid jobs. The Government does not have a program of compulsory education, but it provides universal access to free primary education. More than 98% of school-age children to grade 7 are enrolled in school. In many instances, education for girls is curtailed after having a seventh grade, largely because parents do not allow girls to leave their home island for an island having a secondary school. In 1997, the estimated adult illiteracy rate for the total population was 4.2% for men and 4.3% for women.

For 2000, the rate is 3.7% for men and 3.6% for women, which is an improvement. UNESCO defines an illiterate person as someone who, while understanding the situation, cannot read or write a short, simple statement on his or her everyday life. The crude enrollment rate, which represents the total of inscriptions, regardless of age, for all individuals old enough to attend a particular level. The percentage of parliamentary seats held by women increased between 1995 and 1999, from 2% to 6%. Between 1994 and 1998, the number of women in decision-making positions in government has increase slightly, but women seriously lagged behind in 1998, with 6% of seats at the ministerial level and 11% at the sub-ministerial level.

Gender Equality Council

In October 2000, the Cabinet replaced the national Women's Council with Gender Equality Council to serve as an advisory body to the Government to help strengthen the role of women in society and to help ensure equal participation by women in the country's development.

The Government gives legal literacy programs to make women aware of their legal rights and workshop on gender and political awareness in the outer atolls.

International Conventions for Women There are Four international conferences on gender issues were held between 1975 and 1995. The last one took place in Beijing in 1995 and gathered more than 47,000 representatives from various countries and non-governmental organizations (NGOs). Participants unanimously adopted the Beijing Declaration and the Platform for Action that was in essence an agenda for women's empowerment.

In 1993, Maldives ratified the United-Nations Convention on the Elimination of All Forms of Discrimination Against Women (CEDAW). Following the Fourth World Conference on Women in Beijing, they presented to the United Nations Secretariat their plan to implement the Platform for Action.

Despite the highly dispersed nature of the country that constrains access to health, education, and other social services, the country's social indicators have shown significant improvements. Since 1977, life expectancy at birth increased by over 20 years to 72 years, and infant mortality was reduced from 120 per thousand to 20 by 1999. In education, primary school enrollment increased from 38 percent in 1982 to over 90 percent of the age group, and adult literacy rate reached 98 percent in 1999, which is among the highest in the developing world. Child labour is nonexistent in Maldives. Maldives' population growth rate fell from about 3.4 percent per annum in the 1980s to about 2.7 percent in 1995, but is still considered to be high.

The current population growth imposes a major challenge for Maldives, as it will continue to significantly impact on the future demand for social services (e.g. education, health, water supply and sanitation) and physical infrastructures especially in the outer atolls. Meanwhile, the rapid population growth rate has created a high dependency ratio and a large cohort of young Maldivians are looking for employment.

The Government policy on population consolidation aims to:

(i) establish physical links between islands to improve access of small islands population to better economic and social services, and

(ii) relocate the people from small and remote islands to larger and easily accessible ones to benefit from scale economies in terms of the provision of social and infrastructure services and increased mobility of people and goods.

Malidive island has limited terrestrial resources. Rich marine life and beautiful settings are the mainstay for the development of the fishing and tourism sectors and the sustainable livelihood of the Maldives population. Like many other small island countries, Maldives faces serious environmental problems which include declining freshwater quantity and quality, coastal erosion and pollution, and degradation of coastal resources and the coral reef ecosystem.

The vulnerability of the small island ecosystems is compounded by the threat of the rise in the sea level due to global warming. Most islands are low-lying and about 80 percent of the land area is less than one meter above sea level. The coral growth rate is 3-5 mm per year and has the potential to mitigate some of the effects of sea level rise. However, a study showed that a serious coral bleaching occurred in Maldives in 1998 and caused significant damage to the reefs in the Maldives. The Government, with the assistance of the United Nations Development Programme (UNDP), is monitoring the coral reefs to identify the best approach to manage this fragile ecosystem. In addition, environmental problems associated with improper sanitation practices and over exploitation of the fresh water sources seriously threaten the populated islands.

The Government has recently finalized the Second National Environmental Action Plan following close consultations with the principal stakeholders. The implementation of the Plan remains a major challenge for the Government in view of inadequate funding and limited human resources. Key environmental concerns are being addressed with grant assistance by donor agencies.

Australia, Global Environmental Facility, Japan, and UNDP are providing support in the areas of coastal resources management, environmental infrastructure, the development of an environmental protection strategy, and institutional strengthening. Accordingly, ADB will continue to assist through mainstreaming environmental concerns under its loan and technical assistance (TA) projects. The project preparatory technical assistance (PPTA) for Outer Islands Electrification, being implemented in 2000, will evaluate the feasibility of adopting environmentally sustainable renewable energy sources for electricity generation, such as photovoltaic power, solar thermal and wind power, for the outer islands. ADB has identified critical natural resources and environmental issues to be considered when undertaking development projects in Maldives. Despite strong economic growth in the last two decades, poverty still exists in Maldives. About 74 percent of the Maldives' population reside in the outer islands. Their livelihoods depend on small agriculture, fisheries, and limited public sector employment. Although an official poverty line has not yet been established for Maldives, the recent report by the Government, indicates that income poverty is widespread in Maldives, though with higher incidence in the outer atolls.

About 22 percent of Maldives' population is estimated to be below the income poverty line of Rf10 per person per day ($0.85). The incidence of income poverty rises to 43 percent of the population when based on a higher income poverty line of Rf15 per person per day ($1.27). In Malé, the incidence of poverty for both income poverty lines is less than half of what is found in the outer atolls. The poverty assessment further indicates large differences between Malé and the outer atolls in access to basic social and infrastructure services including education, health, water supply and sanitation, electrification and inter-island transportation services.

The Government accords high priority to the regional development as part of its overall plan to ensure more equitable geographic distribution of economic and social benefits derived from growth. However, it remains a major challenge for the Government to provide adequate essential services for the island populations due to the highly dispersed nature of the country and diseconomies of scale in production, transport, and provision of essential social and infrastructure services.

Establishment of a modern public administration, a comprehensive and transparent set of laws, and an impartial and competent judiciary are emphasized as priority goals in the Government's development agenda. Capacity building and the upgrading of human resources to fill the skills gap have been recognized as critical requirements towards good governance to achieve improved performance of the public and private sectors.

Anti-curruption Bill

The Government will submit an Anti-corruption and Bribery bill for approval by the People's Majlis (Parliament) in 2000, which will broaden the mandate of the Anti-Corruption Board, established in 1991, to also investigate corruption in the private sector. The expansion of the Anti-Corruption Board's mandate would require further improvement in both the quality and quantity of resources made available to the Board.

To this end, an advisory technical assistance (ADTA) for Capacity Building for Good Governance is included in 2003, to provide support to the relevant Government agencies especially in the areas of specialist accounting and auditing to investigate both public and private sector management and accounting related corruption and fraud. Another area of concern is the decentralization of responsibilities for the planning and management of development to the atoll/island levels to build the institutions that could effectively exercise new responsibilities and facilitate the participation of the atoll population in decisions that directly affect the development future of their communities. ADB would continue to support the Government's initiatives in this area through both technical assistance program and investment in regional development project in the medium term.

The current Country Operational Strategy (COS) for Maldives was prepared in 1995 when macroeconomic instability, regional disparities, environmental vulnerability and skill shortages were the major concerns. Accordingly, the operational priorities included:

- improvement of fiscal management;
- promotion of regional development together with improvement of quality of and access to education; and
- the protection of environment.

As the macroeconomic position improved, the Government advised ADB and the International Monetary Fund that it would no longer need external assistance to implement a program of macroeconomic reforms and that it would proceed with the reforms using its own resources. The Government, accordingly, requested ADB to redirect assistance to support improvements in public sector management and human development.

Regional development across atolls has been a high priority for ADB assistance to achieve a more equitable and cost-effective distribution of basic economic and social services and to ease the development pressures on Malé. ADB has approved the Regional Development Project in 1999 aiming at developing a northern development region and a southern development region.

The need for ADB support for human development has remained a high priority. A sustained effort is required to raise the education and skills level of the population to meet the demands of a rapidly modernizing economy and to reduce the heavy reliance on expatriate workers. ADB assisted in the preparation of the Education Sector Master Plan and is currently assisting to restructure and strengthen the postsecondary education system to improve the quality and quantity of skilled manpower in the country.

Success in regional development and the upgrading of human resources will call for strong and sustained commitment and appropriate budget allocations from the Government. Investments in regional development activities will require careful screening to ensure that they are environmentally friendly and cost-effective. With respect to the environment, the Government had been able to mobilize grant assistance from bilateral and multi-lateral sources to address its main concerns.

Accordingly, ADB operations do not include stand-alone environment projects, but address environmental issues in ADB funded projects. Given the logistical challenge of monitoring 199 inhabited and 992 uninhabited islands, over a vast stretch of ocean, this approach is realistic and practical. The preparation work for a new COS/poverty reduction strategy for Maldives commenced in late 1999.

Based on the Vulnerability and Poverty Assessment, ADB is preparing a poverty analysis and a country-specific poverty reduction strategy for Maldives. The poverty reduction strategy will form the basis of a Partnership Agreement between the Government and ADB on poverty reduction in Maldives. The Partnership Agreement, expected to be concluded in 2001, will outline specific operational targets and measures to optimize the poverty impact of the ADB operations in the country and the Government's own commitments to this objective. Close consultation will be conducted with the Government, donors, non-government organizations (NGOs), the private sector, and community groups in formulating the poverty reduction strategy.

The ADB has approved nine loans from its Special Funds resources to Maldives for a total of $55 million, mainly focusing on improvement of power supply and port facilities in Malé. Three loans have been provided in each of the transport and the energy sectors, and one loan each for the education, regional development and multi (mainly energy and ports) sectors. Of the six completed projects, four have been post-evaluated.

Three were rated generally successful with notably good project design. The one unsuccessful project was Loan 513-MLD: Interisland Transport Project, approved in 1981 for $1 million. It suffered from major project design flaws. The 37 TAs provided by ADB have had a wider sectoral coverage than the loan program, and included assistance for national planning, financial sector development, and improved public sector management and good governance. Ten TAs were for the preparation of loan projects and 27 TAs were for advisory activities.

ADB assistance enabled a reliable electric power supply and significantly improved port operations in Malé. ADB assistance has also supported human development and institutional capacity building in these two sectors, as the shortage of technical experts in engineering, finance, accounting, planning and management has been a key constraint.

The corporatization of the public power utility in 1997 and the Maldives Port Authority (MPA), being implemented in 2000, were among significant achievements. Recent ADB lending operations put emphasis on more equitable growth across atolls through the promotion of regional development.

The Regional Development Project in 1999 is the first project that directly promotes the Government's strategy for regional development through the provision of basic infrastructure and services and institutional support. ADB technical assistance has also been provided in the area of development planning and this has helped the Government identify key development issues and formulate medium- and long-term national plans. These plans have guided economic and social development planning and have also provided a consistent policy framework for identifying development priorities.

In recent years the ADB's TA program has been effective in assisting the Government to:

- develop national accounting skills;
- strengthen the operational efficiency of the Audit Office and enhance capacity of public accounting system;
- improve institutional arrangements for the postsecondary education system;
- promote private sector participation in port operations;
- strengthen legal education and judicial training; and
- develop science and technology masterplan.

The ADB's loan portfolio in Maldives comprises only three active loans, as a result of which disbursement ratios tend to vary depending on the stage of project implementation. However, past implementation experience indicates delays have occurred primarily in the initial phases of project implementation in the appointment of consultants, procurement, and contract award.

Procurement for public sector project following international competitive bidding was institutionalized only in 1997, when a committee was formulated consisting of staff from Ministry of Finance and Treasury, the Audit Office, and the concerned project agency to undertake preparation of bid documents and tender evaluation. The lack of qualified and experienced technical staff in the procurement committee has so far resulted in heavy reliance on international consultants for procurement work in these islands.

The current practice is neither cost-effective due to the high costs of contracting consultants nor sustainable as the Government has limited involvement in and understanding of the required legal and technical specifications of the tender document. Accordingly, a small-scale technical assistance for Procurement Support and Project Management is included in 2000, to strengthen the capacity of procurement staff in preparation of bidding documents, evaluation of tender documents and project management and monitoring, to enhance the effectiveness of Government procurement procedures. Performance-based Allocation (PBA), as being currently designed, uses both top-down and bottom-up approaches in evaluating country performance. Common standardized criteria across all borrowers comprising, e.g., economic growth, or monetary policy stance, is an example of a top down criteria; while specific tariff adjustment, or a specific policy reform in borrower's economy, or portfolio management would be examples of a bottom-up approach.

Under the proposed system, country specific allocation will depend upon the borrower's per capita gross national product (GNP), the size of its population, and performance of its economy. The factors that will be critical in determining country specific performance in Maldives relate to:

- macroeconomic management;
- structural policies;
- poverty reduction policies;
- protection of environment;
- governance and public sector management; and
- portfolio performance.

At the same time, it should be noted that Maldives will be treated as special case together with the Pacific developing member countries for the relatively small size of the country and the vulnerability of its economy to external shocks. The development of specific indicators to measure country performance is expected to be complete by the end of 2000, in extensive consultations with key Government agencies, policy institutes, and other donors.

While some criteria are based on objective quantitative indicators and some others are subjective in nature, the PBA assessment is also based on both immediate past performance and the promise of future performance. Asian Development Bank (ADB) has made significant contribution through its loan and TA program to help meet the electricity demands in Malé and to undertake institutional development of the power sector. The Third Power System Development Project has been geared to improving the reliability of the power supply in Malé.

The Government's Fifth National Development Plan and ADB's poverty reduction strategy both call for the shifting of future development projects in the sector to the outer atolls, where the majority of the country's poor reside and the economic and social development has been constrained by poor electricity supply. While significant progress has been made in atoll electrification, about 28 percent of the atoll population reportedly have electricity for 6 hours or less each day: the quality is poor and the costs are usually high.

This restricts their income earning activities. Planned assistance by ADB during 2001-2003 includes a loan project for Outer Islands Electrification in 2001, to be prepared by a PPTA being implemented in 2000, aiming to provide environmentally sustainable sources of energy for the outer island population and to improve governance of the sector.

In the absence of comprehensive strategy and planning in the transport sector, the sector development has been undertaken in a relatively ad hoc manner, which has resulted in the inefficiency of investment projects and the lack of coordination in external assistance.

The Government expressed its strong desire to formulate the first National Transport Master Plan, covering international sea transport and inter-islands shipping, air transportation networks and road transport. An ADTA for Transport Master Plan is included in 2001, to assist the Government to develop a master plan for the transport sector together with a strategic environmental impact study. To further support its regional development plan by providing basic infrastructure and social services to create economic opportunities for the island population, a PPTA for Islands Roads Development has been included in 2002, focusing on selected regional development centers for synergy effect on regional development impact, of course in a beneficial way.

One of the major deficiencies in the financial sector is non-availability of long-term finance. Lending capacity of domestic commercial banks is not adequate to meet the financial needs of the private sector, especially resort development projects in the tourism subsector. The importance of capital market developments as an alternative measure to mobilize medium and long-term financing of capital investment has been recognized. ADB is conducting a comprehensive review of the financial sector and has formulated a paper on Strategic Thrust on the Financial Sector for Maldives. ADB will continue to dialogue with the Government on possible assistance to further reforms in the financial sector in future.

Human resource development is a high priority, with two distinct goals: to sustain higher economic growth and to address regional disparities between the outer islands and the Malé region. The dearth of sufficiently skilled workers is a serious obstacle to achieving national development objectives, and continued efforts in human resource development will be required to reduce the dependence on expatriate labor and save foreign exchange. The strategy for human resource development needs to further target quality improvement through curriculum development, expansion of secondary education and distant learning, and skill development through vocational training.

The Government has taken steps to strengthen the education system, with particular emphasis on improving the capacity of the postsecondary education system. Through the ongoing Postsecondary Education Development Project, ADB is assisting the Government in strengthening the management and expanding the output of the postsecondary education system by improving the seven existing technical institutes under the Maldives College of Higher Education (MCHE). Postsecondary Education Development is planned for 2002, to be prepared by a PPTA in 2001, focusing on outreach programs to the atolls to ensure that education and training become available to students on the atolls. The Government emphasized that both secondary and postsecondary education need to be further developed to address critical skill shortages to meet the urgent need for key economic and social sector developments in the atolls as part of the country's regional development plan.

In this respect, an ADTA for Tertiary Education in Outer

Atolls is also included in 2002, providing support for development and implementation of outreach tertiary education programs for the atolls. The newly established Tertiary Institute for Open Learning is expected to especially benefit from the institutional capacity building support provided under the ADTA. With limited land, natural resources, skilled labor and capital, Maldives has been seeking ways to take advantage of science, information and technology to promote sustainable economic growth while reducing dependency on tourism and fisheries.

The ongoing TA for Science and Technology Masterplan has been supporting the Government to develop a science and technology masterplan which would provide a strategy and action plan for the country's science and technological development, and to strengthen the capacity of the newly established Ministry of Communication, Science and Technology.

Provision for investment support for Information Technology Development in both Malé and the outer atolls has been made in 2001 following completion of the TA for Science and Technology Masterplan by the end of 2000. The development of information network would support the development of a modern economy with increased focus on services industry, and especially, it would improve public sector management efficiency, transparency, and accountability, and facilitate the Government's decentralization programs to empower local decision-makings in support of regional development. The development of information network would improve public information to build consensus and ignite community pressures to promote responsible behavior towards the environment.

Regional disparity between Malé and the outer islands has continued to be a key development issue. The average per capita income differential between the Malé region and poorer outer islands is estimated at 3:1. In addition, there is also a marked discrepancy between Malé and the outer islands in the availability of physical and social infrastructure such as schools, markets, health care facilities, sanitation and energy.

The rapid growth of the population in Maldives has increased the urgency for the provision of a broad range of economic and social infrastructure in the outer islands. The wide dispersal of the population inevitably raises the costs in providing these services. Meanwhile, it is recognized that an excessive development focus on the Malé region will constrain future growth. Therefore regional development is considered to be a key factor in easing the development pressures on Malé and at the same time addressing equity concerns.

The Government acknowledges the recent assistance extended by ADB in promoting regional development in the northern and southern regional development centers. Under the Regional Development Project, a program to develop a northern development region and a southern development region including establishment of two Regional Development and Management Offices (RDMOs) in the two regions will be implemented.

Overall progress of the ongoing Project has been satisfactory, and construction for the two permanent RDMOs buildings, one in the northern development region and one in the southern development region, will be completed in 2000. However, the RDMOs are already in operation in a rented accommodation since the commencement of the Project in May 2000.

Following the Government's strong request to start early preparation of a second phase regional development, focusing on development of the northern central and southern central regions, a PPTA for Second Regional Development has been included in 2001, which would enable the Government to seek co-financing opportunity from other donors based on the investment proposal. A loan project is planned in 2003, following satisfactory progress of the ongoing Regional Development Project.

The Government has recently taken steps to mainstream gender issues to ensure a balanced development. It initiated workshops promoting awareness and legal literacy among women and increasing their participation in the decision making process in the community and the public and private sectors. In the outer islands, ADB's operational program has been assisting gender development through increasing women's access to education and training.

Regional Development Project

ADB's Regional Development Project is also expected to

mitigate the pressure on male out-migration to the Malé region that has resulted in a high incidence of female-headed households in the outer islands. ADB will assist the Government to conduct a gender participatory assessment, which will evaluate the effectiveness of the institutional mechanisms for formulating and implementing gender and development policies and programs, and develop a strategy of gender-sensitive policies.

The Maldives is presently going through the initial stage of the demographic transitionwith high fertility and low mortality, and a growth rate of 2.8 per cent. At the present rateof growth, the population will double by the year 2015. With limited availability of Iand,this growth would produce a population density that would be comparable to those found in countries with high population concentrations. Therefore accommodating the growingpopulation, and achieving stabilization, are the dual challenges facing the Maldives. Maldives views population issues as an integral part of overall development. As such,many of the goals and objectives of ICPD find expression in the goals and objectives ofnational development plans. And the provision of health and education, housing, incomeand employment as well as environmental management becomes crucial elements of thecountry's population strategy.

The government recognizes the critical importance of thepeople's participation in developin, and implementing national strategies, and stronglyencourages the active involvement of NGOs and community based organisations in thisprocess. Since ICPD Maldives has taken many initiatives in further strengthening theholistic nature of their population policy.

In the sameway, the changing nature of the family structure, which is becoming increasinglynuclearised, is fully recognised in formulating population strategies. These changes haveimportant implications for the role of women within, and out side the family. And, effortsare being made to empower them to make informed decisions with respect to theirreproductive health, careers, and family life. The reproductive health approach of theMaldives emphasises a life cycle perspective, where awareness, and educationprogrammes seek to raise the age of marriage, provide counseling on youth andadolescent problems.

Role of U.N.

At the United Nations World Conference Against Racism, Racial Discrimination, Xenophobia and Related Intolerance (WCAR), women's rights activists successfully worked to have the final document reflect how sex and race intersected to render women vulnerable to sexual violence in armed conflict and to trafficking, and reinforced women's right to transfer their nationality, on an equal basis with men, to their children.

As states and nongovernmental organisations (NGOs) throughout the world prepared for the WCAR, women's human rights activists explored the intersection between race, ethnicity, or religion and gender and the impact of this intersection on women's ability to enjoy human rights and fundamental freedoms.

Women experienced racism and sexism not as separate events but as violations that were mutually reinforcing. For example, soldiers and noncombatants subjected women to sexual violence in armed conflict not just because they were women but also because they were women of a particular race, nationality, ethnicity, or religion. Indeed, armed factions often portrayed acts of sexual violence against women in conflict zones as attacks on the entire community, a community typically identified by a shared race, religion or ethnicity. Likewise, women were vulnerable to trafficking into forced labor, not just because they were poor and uneducated, but also because in many countries their poverty and illiteracy was a function of discrimination against women of a particular race, ethnicity, or religion. But the impact of this convergence of racism and sexism did not end with women experiencing trafficking-related human rights violations; it also affected how government officials, such as police and prosecutors, in both sending and receiving countries perceived them. Governments treated trafficked women as illegal immigrants at best, criminals at worst.

Women experienced widespread violations of labor rights because of their race and gender. In some cases, states created such varied categories of workers that some women were unable to prove discrimination compared to women of different races. They were also unable to prove discrimination compared to men of the same race. In the US manufacturing sector, white women may be employed in the front offices as secretaries and receptionists while black men may be employed in the factory, making it impossible for black women to prove discrimination because the employer hires women and hires blacks. But states did not just violate women's rights in the public sphere; they also persisted in enforcing laws and condoning practices that discriminated against women in the private sphere.

Governments defended these discriminatory laws and practices as essential to maintaining the integrity of religion and culture. Numerous governments, as in Morocco and Peru, continued to uphold laws that gave women inferior legal status within the family and that violated women's rights to change or retain their nationality.

Some countries, such as Syria and Malaysia, violated women's right to enter into marriage with their free and full consent as well as their right to dissolve a marriage on an equal basis with men. The motivation behind these discriminatory laws appeared to be to keep women from marrying men of a different nationality, ethnicity, or religion. While the type of discrimination varied from region to region, women throughout the world found that their relationship to a male relative or husband determined their rights.

3

Social Status

The Maldives society is relatively homogenous, connected by two bonds of language and religion. Islam was introduced to the Maldives in the 12th century and in 1155 the entire nation was converted after the royal decree of the king who took the title of "Sultan." In addition to the local language, Dhivehi, which is spoken throughout the country, English is also widely used and is fairly popular medium of instruction in schools. This has helped students from the Maldives to access higher education in neighboring countries in South Asia as well as other countries such as Australia, New Zealand, Singapore, Malaysia and the United Kingdom.

Education Master Plan

In 1995, during the preparation of the Education Master Plan, the use of Dhivehi as a medium of instruction at the primary level was proposed. However, discussions with parents at the atoll level clearly pointed to a preference by parents and teachers to keep English as the medium of instruction, with Dhivehi being taught as a second language and as the medium of instruction for teaching Islam (religious studies). Though the traditional kinship system is patrilineal, early historical records reveal the existence of female rulers and instances of inheritance of power through the female line. The succession to the throne was maybe originally to younger brothers of the king and, in the absence of brothers, to a daughter and her sister as in the Sri Lankan dynasties.

The common man and women take great pride in its uniqueness and is greatly influenced by traditional values, such as a preference for the extended family system.

Traditional Maldivian society was stratified at the beginning of the 20th century into the royalty, upper class, middle class, and local class. This stratification is no longer well defined due to the social mobility made possible by the spread of education and promotions in the private and government sectors. There are three different levels of address in the Maldivian language even today: one for the royalty and the upper classes, including officials; another for the middle classes; and a third way of addressing local classes. A fourth informal form is used for conversation with close friends, one's children and sometimes younger members of the family. Respect for parents and elders of the family are very important values and hence children from all levels address their parents and elders respectfully in the upper or middle forms of address. Professionals such as teachers and doctors, magistrates, high government officials and community leaders are also addressed in the higher forms of address.

The Maldives is traditionally a seafaring nation. Men usually go out to the sea to fish; the women help in cooking and smoking of fish. The latter has developed into a cottage industry. In the few farming islands, the men plough and till the fields while women help with the planting of seeds and harvesting of crops. As men spend long hours at sea, it is the traditional role of women to look after the children and the home. At present there is one woman in the Cabinet and five women in the Parliament. However, even after three decades of development, there are very few women in high-level positions both in the government and private sectors. The society in the Maldives is, by and large, dominated by males, particularly in senior government positions. Women, however, enjoy several rights in their day-to-day lives as compared with their counterparts in many other Islamic countries in the region. They have a high degree of physical and social mobility, equal right and access to education and health services, and the freedom to select or divorce their spouses.

The well-known writings of ancient sources such as *Al-Idrisi* (who lived 1099-1168) and the famous traveller Ibn Batuta evidence ancient roots of the liberal atmosphere prevailing today with regard to gender relations. To quote Al-Idrisi, "All these islands have a chief (*ra'is*) who unites them, protects and defends them, and makes truce according to his ability. His wife acts as an arbitrator among the people and does not veil herself from them. When she issues her orders, her husband, the chief, though he is present, does not interfere with any of her ordinances. It has always been a custom with them that a woman arbitrate, a custom which they do not depart." Ibn Batuta writes, "Their womenfolk do not cover their heads, not even their queen does so, and they comb their hair and gather it at one side."

In 1995, during the preparation of the Education Master Plan, the use of Dhivehi as a medium of instruction at the primary level was proposed. However, discussions with parents at the atoll level clearly pointed to a preference by parents and teachers to keep English as the medium of instruction, with Dhivehi being taught as a second language and as the medium of instruction for teaching Islamic principles. The first formal school for boys started in male in the 1920s and for girls some 20 years later in 1944 as a branch of the boys' school. So men have clearly had a head start in education over women. However, "modern" English education for boys and girls was introduced at the same time in the 1960s. As women pursue higher education at home and overseas, the number of women who have a college education is gradually increasing. Since they were able to get the same education as men, women started joining government offices and were paid as much as the men for the same jobs.

Today, even though women have attained higher levels of education and some success with careers, it has become very difficult for them to balance career development and success with caring for children and families. With the traditional extended family support in child-rearing slowly disappearing and no organised child-care facilities available to replace this system, it is a big challenge for women to balance a successful job or career and manage their families simultaneously. This is certainly one factor that would hinder women from contributing equally as men in senior posts in the government and private sectors. In the 1995 census, the economically active Maldivian population numbered 66,887, a 3.1 per cent per annum growth in the 1990-1995 inter-censal period.

During the same period, the number of foreign nationals

working in the Maldives grew by an annual rate of 16.5 per cent. Foreign nationals comprised 21.7 per cent of the total workforce in 1995 and their participation in the labor force has increased more than threefold from 1988 to 1996. The LFPR of the Maldivians aged 15-64 is just under 50 per cent. Even if Maldivians replaced all foreign nationals, it would still be below 70 per cent. The reasons for the relatively low LFPR is to be carefully examined by the Government in the Plan period and strategies put in place to address the situation.The women of the Maldives are among the most emancipated in the Islamic world. Overt sex-based discrimination is not a part of the Maldivian psyche. While there is no evidence of a strong women's movement in the past, it is gaining momentum now as gender disparities and constraints in women's development become more visible as a consequence of the rapid development of the economy, primarily in sectors that offer limited opportunities for women's participation and due to the changing social scenario in the Republic. The important role that women traditionally played in the economy has perhaps been eroded, especially in the fisheries sector, due to rapid mechanisation and changes in fish preservation and marketing techniques. Besides, social restrictions on women's mobility interfere with their optimal participation in the expanding tourism industry.

The improvement in mortality rates during the last two decades has helped to increase the life expectancy of women from 48 years in 1978 to 72 years in 1995, as compared to the corresponding age of 70 years for males. This came down marginally in 1997 to 70.15 and 69.2, respectively. Significantly, there is no dramatic variation between the rural and urban life expectancy figures, as is the pattern in other developing countries. This is indicative of the equitable access to health services that women enjoy in both male and the atolls.

The UNDP Vulnerability and Poverty Assessment Survey that covered all the 200 inhabited islands in the Maldives found no evidence of any discrimination against girl children in terms of their access to health services. On the contrary, the IMRs among boys were observed to be higher than those for girls. This conforms to the latest global trends, the reasons for which are still not clear.

The Survey

The survey found the IMRs to be consistently higher for boys than for girls without a single exception. Although both the sexes have equal access to health services, the health of women reportedly tends to be inferior to that of men in the atoll and island communities that are distant from health centres, perhaps due to constraints of travel to the health centre. Some of the main difficulties encountered by the Maldivian women relate to child-bearing, with women in the atoll communities giving birth to an average of six children in the course of their reproductive lives. This high fertility rate is particularly prevalent among women in the islands that are further away from male. In these remote islands there is a significant gap between the desired and actual number of births, which stand at about 3 and 6.4, respectively.

One of the factors of the high fertility rate could perhaps be related to the high rate of divorce and remarriage in the country. It is likely that women come under considerable social pressure to produce offspring from each of their marriages. The incidence of contraceptive use is as low as 18 per cent as compared with India, for instance, which has a corresponding rate of 45 per cent. The participation in and support to family planning measures by men is extremely low, with contraceptive use rates hovering below 20 per cent for males as compared with over 80 per cent for women. It is imperative to change this situation by focusing on educating men to check the rapid growth of population as well as to control the rising incidence of HIV and AIDS infections in the region.

Analmia is highly prevalent among pregnant mothers and women. More than 60 per cent of the pregnant women suffer from analmia. Eight per cent of the women are below the cut-off point laid down by WHO for mean haemoglobin levels for women. The frequency of multiple births without adequate spacing between them is probably one of the factors responsible for this poor health status among the Maldivian women.The data on live births indicates a fall in the number of births from 6,101 in 1997 to 5,675 in 1998. Alarmingly, this number increased in the very young age group of 10-14 years from 3 to 12 within the same period, that is, it went up from a negligible level to 0.21 per cent.

The Government has been actively promoting the use of contraceptives and had set a target of reaching a contraceptive prevalence rate (CPR) of 30 per cent by 1996. However, the national user prevalence increased from a low rate of 10 per cent for 1993, to only 16.6 per cent in 1996 and went up marginally to 18.5 per cent by 1998. The data do not capture the use of the conventional methods of family planning. There are also considerable variations in CPRs between various atolls, ranging from a low of 7.4 per cent to a high of 34.1 per cent. However, the knowledge of at least one method of contraception is nearly universal and the attitude towards birth control among the local communities is also very positive, according to the Knowledge, Attitude and Practice study conducted in 1991. Over 40 per cent of the women wanted no more children, while 50 per cent felt that there should be at least a two-year gap between pregnancies and over 40 per cent reported that their last pregnancy had not been planned. The ideal family size was believed to consist of an average of 4.3 children. The reasons have more to do with limited knowledge among the users and inadequate availability of related health services.

In fact no large-scale surveys were undertaken until the 1990s to assess the nutritional status of the population in the Maldives. In 1994, the Ministry of Health and Family Welfare conducted a national survey in collaboration with WHO and UNICEF, but it covered only 5 per cent of the total households in the country. The results of these studies revealed that 16 per cent of the children under five years of age were suffering from moderate to severe wasting, 30 per cent had moderate to severe stunting, and approximately 38 per cent were underweight.

The limited data available from previous studies shows that the occurrence of severe malnutrition among children has not decreased since 1985. This is mainly due to the prevalence of poor feeding practices. There is no extensive data on nutrition trends in the country. Although growth monitoring is carried out regularly among children of up to three years of age, wherein over 95 per cent of the target population is covered, it does not seem to have had any significant repercussions for children who falter in growth. It has been observed that when growth faltering occurs, no attempts are made by the health workers to take special care of the affected children or to counsel the mothers concerned.

Anemia is a major public health problem in the country. Approximately 82 per cent of the children, 68 per cent of the pregnant women and 62 per cent of the non-pregnant women suffer from anemia. As a result, parasitic infestation is widely prevalent. Thalassemia constitutes another major problem in the Maldives, with approximately 18 per cent of the population reported to be carriers of the disease. There is no information on the dietary intake of iron and its bioavailability. Ninety-five per cent of the deliveries are conducted by trained personnel and the incidence of low birth weight is 20 per cent. In accordance with the findings of the United Nations Children's Fund (UNICEF) in 1995, the rate of occurrence of goiter among school children is 23 per cent. Intervention strategies are thus being evolved currently, prescribing the required amount of iodine through iodised salt for human consumption. Data on the status of vitamin A intake is not available. However, related indirect indicators such as nutritional status concerning breast-feeding patterns, anthropometric measurements, prevalence of low birth weight, availability of food in the markets and households, and incidence of parasitic and other infections suggest that the occurrence of subclinical Vitamin A deficiency among the local population is likely. For this reason, a national survey on Vitamin A status was recommended by the WHO Regional Office in the Maldives, about 8 per cent of the infants are exclusively breast-fed from birth to at least up to three months of age and in the rural areas, breast-feeding is often continued for one year. Breast milk substitutes are, however, introduced to infants in the urban areas as early as at the age of one month. The traditional weaning foods are millet gruel and legumes. It is unfortunate that fish, which is available in the country in abundance, is not commonly used in child feeding, which could alleviate malnutrition in children under 5 years. The Maldives has also not adopted the international code of marketing for breast milk substitutes.

The delivery of health services and related communication is often affected by geographical constraints. The food security and the flow of food products to the remote islands that have no agricultural production are vulnerable to bad weather conditions. Food sufficiency is dependent on imported food, and distribution channels are controlled by the private sector. Fruits and vegetables do not generally figure in the common Maldivian diet. As per the food production index, there is a shortfall to the extent of 10 per cent in the country's food production and the daily energy supply, as per the present requirement, falls short by 13 per cent.

Food Consumption

There is a need for building a good database on food consumption trends and the nutritional status of the population. It has been observed that children's weights are recorded regularly but the health workers do not take any action in cases where growth faltering occurs. This activity, therefore, needs to be constantly supervised and staff needs to be properly trained to ensure adequate nutrition among the children. For this purpose, training institutes need to be established and promoted for developing an efficient cadre of personnel to effectively handle the country's nutrition programs at all levels.

A total of 1,425 children in the atolls and 250 children in male were measured for height, weight and arm circumference by the survey enumerators of the 1998 Vulnerability and Poverty Assessment. The data obtained were analysed with the assistance of UNICEF by using special software to assess the extent of both wasting and stunting among the children. Wasting and stunting were considered to exist when observations fell outside of two standard deviations from the distribution applicable to the world population.

Although the above revelations should be regarded as approximations rather than hard facts, they are a genuine cause for concern. In the case of wasting, prevalence rates of 8-15 per cent are not uncommon among children in many developing countries. However, prevalence rates in excess of 15 per cent are usually indicative of the seriousness of the situation. These figures for the Maldives are far higher than the danger level, both for stunting and wasting. A comparison of the survey's results with other data on malnutrition in the Maldives supports the view that there has been no significant improvement in this area in the last 16 years. On the contrary, the available evidence points to an overall worsening of the situation, which can be attributed to a range of factors including faulty dietary habits and preferences, poor infant and child-care practices, and the high incidence of diseases like diarrhea, acute respiratory infection and worm infestation. The incidence of acute anemia among many mothers, partly attributable to hookworm infestation, is also an important causative factor for the alarming health situation. Despite the fact that the Maldives is a small country with limited technical know how and resources, it is extremely appreciable that several of the diseases that result in high morbidity in the neighboring countries of Bangladesh, India, Nepal and Pakistan have either been eradicated here or have very low transmission rates. Even dreaded diseases such as malaria, tuberculosis and leprosy have been controlled at manageable levels.

Only 10 HIV positive cases were reported in the Maldives until 1998. However, anecdotal evidence points to an increasing trend in the detection of positive cases, which are perhaps not reported. There is only one hospital in male that is equipped to conduct the necessary tests for detection of HIV.

An official recognition of drug abuse problem in Maldives came in 1977, and the first legislation was passed the same year. Subsequently it was amended in 1995 to distinguish between illegal drug suppliers and consumers. The former are punished severely, but the latter now have the opportunity for rehabilitation at the only centre set up for the purpose, equipped with trained staff, on Himmafushi Island close to male. In June 2000, 144 persons participated in the rehabilitation programme, of which 15 were women. The youngest client was only 13 years old.

Second time arrests for drug abuse, however, preclude the option of rehabilitation and the offender is instead given a 15-year jail term. The increasing population pressures, resulting in overcrowding particularly in male and the rapid changes in society due to changing occupations and the breakdown of the joint family system, have all contributed to the increasing drug abuse. The rise from one case in 1977 to 235 cases in 1998, in the 16-24 age group, is certainly a cause for concern in the islands.

The overall national figures indicating the people's access

to safe drinking water and sanitation facilities are quite high. National statistics quote a figure of 92 per cent for drinking water. But other estimates place the figure at 82 per cent for water and 84 per cent for sanitation coverage. An analysis of the drinking water situation was also made a part of the 1998 Vulnerability and Poverty Assessment. It was reported that the Maldivian society traditionally depends on shallow wells for access to the islands' freshwater lens and that these wells are now increasingly polluted, especially due to the percolation of human wastes below the earth's surface largely caused by the introduction of modern methods of sanitation with soak pits. Further excessive mining of groundwater has resulted in salinity intrusion, and desalination plants have become a necessity on the islands, or else they may eventually become unfit for human habitation.

In recognition of this problem and the declining quality of well water in many islands, high priority has been accorded to the construction of both collective and individual rainwater tanks and rainwater collection schemes, with the aim of ensuring that the atoll population has access to at least two litres of rainwater per person per day.

This policy has greatly facilitated the shift from usage of well water to rainwater in many islands. Rainwater tanks, both concrete and PVC ones, which are finding increasing usage, are a familiar sight in many island schools and health centres. The management and cleanliness of these tanks is often overseen by members of the women's development committee.

The Vulnerability and Poverty Assessment makes it quite clear that in almost all atolls, rainwater is now more widely used than well water as the main source of drinking water. The Government considers properly stored rainwater to be safe for human consumption, except during the occurrence of epidemics. In accordance with this position, rainwater, regardless of whether it has been treated prior to use or not, has been considered safe for consumption. Unsafe water is defined as untreated well water. In keeping with this definition, the Survey estimates that nine per cent of the population has no access to safe potable water, with this figure increasing to 12 per cent in the case of the atoll population.

Water shortages constitute a more serious problem than the lack of access to safe drinking water. According to the

Survey, one quarter of the atoll population experienced periods during the previous year when there were insufficient supplies of drinking water. The shortage was particularly pronounced in some southern atolls including Alif Dhekunu Buri, Vaavu, Gnaviyani and Meemu, where almost one half of the population experienced shortages of drinking water. In male, most households are connected to a closed sewerage system in which sewage is disposed of through outlet pipes to the sea. Although the situation in the atolls shows a marked improvement in this area, most households are still dependent upon more traditional methods of waste disposal. An indication of the improvements recorded can be obtained by comparing the results of the 1998 Vulnerability and Poverty Assessment with the results of the 1990 Population and Housing Census.

The comparison proves that the percentage of the population without access to toilet facilities decreased from more than 60 per cent to 20 per cent during the said period. This improvement was witnessed in all the atolls with the exception of Seenu, where the percentage of the population without access to sanitation facilities appears to have increased from 10 per cent to 15 per cent over the eight-year period under study. More than one half of the atoll population uses the available toilet facilities and one in four members of the population makes use of an open area surrounded by walls (*gifili*). The situation appears to be most conducive for proper sanitation in the atolls in the central and north central zones, where more than 80 per cent of the population has access to toilet facilities. One in five of all persons in the atolls, however, still has no access to any kind of toilet facility. Although the sanitation situation is improving, the growth of toilet facilities for the atoll population may signify only marginal improvements for environmental health. Many of the toilet facilities, including the traditional ones, discharge gifili sewage and human wastes into the groundwater. This groundwater is still used in many islands for cooking, washing and even as drinking water.

The Maldivians have traditionally placed a high value on and given priority to education. Regardless of their sex, all the children attend school and acquire the basic skills of reading and writing Dhivehi as well as Arabic and religious education.

The public demand for basic education continues to be very strong. The foundations for the near universal primary level education and increasing opportunities for secondary and post-secondary education as well as attempts to provide tertiary and technical training were perhaps laid by this strong tradition of learning in the country. But howsoever impressive may be the gains in the education sector, the Government cannot afford to be complacent, especially on issues of access to higher education for children from the atolls, particularly girls. There is also a need to strengthen the indigenous resource of well-trained teachers to cater to the expanding education sector and reduce reliance on expatriate teachers for sustaining the gains made in this sector in the past three decades. The formal school system consists of government schools, community schools and a few private schools. In 1998, community schools accounted for 43 per cent of the seats in the Republic and 48 per cent in the atolls. Government-run schools, on the other hand, accounted for 41 per cent and 12 per cent were run by private organisations. The Government is gradually taking over the community schools and upgrading the infrastructure while also trying to improve the teacher/ student ratio. An Education Master Plan for 1995-2000 was prepared with Asian Development Bank (ADB) assistance to guide investments in the sector. The Education Development Centre has been paying careful attention to gender equality in producing textbooks for the national primary school curriculum since 1984.

Adult Literacy

The Maldives recorded an adult literacy rate of 87 per cent as early as 1970, much higher than the average of 48 per cent for developing countries. By 1998, its adult literacy rate was 98 per cent, comparable to those prevailing in developed countries. While English education started much later, a very high percentage of Maldivians today are able to read and write their own language, Dhivehi. There is an increasing trend in enrollment for higher education over the period 1990- 1999, with a 60 per cent growth from 62,946 in 1990 to 101,081 in 1999 for the Republic as a whole. But there is a markedly contrasting trend between Male and the atolls. In male there has been stagnation in enrollment, while in the atolls, enrollment went up by 74 per cent during the 1990s, perhaps due to better facilities having been created in the atolls.

In fact until 1985, the opportunity to complete primary education up to Grade VII was available only in the capital, Male, as a result of which the number of girls completing primary school was less than boys. Arranging travel to and accommodation in Male is more difficult for girls than for boys. However, it was after 1990 when Grade VII education became available in the atoll schools that the enrollment of girls for secondary education increased; in fact the enrollment of girls in Grades VIII, IX and X is slightly higher for girls both in the atolls and in male. There are equal opportunities for participation in extracurricular and co-curricular activities for both boys and girls. The composition of enrollment in different kind of institutions has also undergone a change from 1990 to 1999. The share of government institutions in the total enrollment has increased from 39 per cent to 49 per cent, while the combined share of community and private institutions has fallen during this period. This is because the Government is gradually taking over the community schools in an effort to upgrade them and bring about some uniformity in the level of education on the islands that had so far pursued an education policy in keeping with their financial status.

A comparison of the percentage shares of males and females in the total enrollment for all grades for the period 1996-1999 shows a constant share of 51 per cent for males and 49 per cent for females over this four-year period. The percentage share of females in the total enrollment has increased for all grades over these four years except for the primary grade where it has declined. A distinct difference is observed in this regard between male and the atolls. While the enrollment is fairly stable across all grades for the former, for the latter there is a sharp drop in enrollment after Grade VII and another sharp drop after Grade X. This implies that very few Maldivians living in the atolls go in for higher education.

The Government has been offering a few scholarships to enable the island children to pursue secondary education at the Southern Secondary School (SSS) since 1998. These are open to students of the islands, which do not have facilities for secondary education, with equal opportunities for both boys and girls.The accessibility to schools appears to be the greatest impediment for island children pursuing secondary and/or higher education. Some of the remote islands in the atolls still do not have secondary education facilities. No matter how bright the students may be, if they do not have secondary schools in their home islands, they cannot obtain secondary education unless they go to another island or atoll where it is available.

Travelling to other islands in the same atoll or to another atoll coupled with boarding and lodging involves high costs and the aspiring students often find it difficult to get accommodation in the capital Male and the two islands of Seenu Hithadhoo and Haa-Dhaal Kuludufushi, which have the southern and northern regional schools, respectively. Several other atolls now have opportunities for secondary education as well. However, even if a student were to travel to another island to enrol, accommodation has to be arranged on a home-stay basis. This has its own problems.

Practical Problem

Therefore, parents tend to hesitate in sending girl-children outside their home islands. More than 80 per cent of the students in the three largest co-educational schools in Male, namely, EPSS, MES and Ahmedhiyya School, are from the other islands. Each of the 20 atolls have atoll education centres (AECs) and at least two schools provide secondary education. Most of these AECs provide education up to the Grade X level.

The students have the opportunity of appearing for overseas exams, that is, the GCE ordinary level exams of the University of London Schools Examination Board, and the CPE and FCE (English exams) of the Cambridge University Examination Board. Since no arrangements were made for the atoll students to pursue A-Level studies, only those students who could afford to travel to the capital male and got accommodation there eventually got the chance to study for the GCE A-Level examination. However, it is proposed to start A-Level studies in 2001 in Baa AEC in Kydhafushi; Southern Secondary School (now Muhibbuddin School) in S. Hithadhoo would be starting A-Level studies in 2001; and Northern Secondary School (now Jalaaluddin School) in H.Dh. Kulhuddhufishi will start A-Level studies within the next few years. These constraints pose similar problems for both boys and girls.

In 2000, three female students from SSS who got admission to the highly competitive Science Education Centre (the only government institution with formal A-Level classes) could not attend classes, because they could not get accommodation in Male. The only logical solution to this problem appears to be to i) start A-Level classes in the regional schools of SSS and Northern Secondary School in 2001 in the near future, as planned, and to start these classes in AECs in the other atolls in the distant future; and ii) to provide boarding facilities for students in the two regional schools in the near future, and in AECs in the other atolls in the distant future.Youth and adults who have not been able to profit from the formal education system are provided with opportunities to complete extended basic education at an accelerated rate through non-formal education. Under the Condensed Education program implemented by the Non-Formal Education Centre (NFEC), out-of-school youth and people beyond school age can complete Grades I-VII in three years.

The course is usually offered at an AEC and is usually taught by primary teachers in the evenings. The NFEC also conducts courses in Thaana and Arabic Calligraphy, Dhivehi, and Thaana Typing. Short skills development programmes including Embroidery and Sewing, First Aid and Carpentry are also conducted. Other institutions such as the Institute of Health Sciences, the Institute of Hotel and Catering Services and the Maldivian Institute of Technical Education also conduct short-term vocational education programs. In 1999, 349 students participated in various education programs of NFEC; of these 245 (70 per cent) were women. Non-formal educational programs, particularly in the fields of population and health education, are targeted at students of primary and secondary schools, out-of-school youth, teachers and community leaders and adults.

The Literacy and Neo-Literacy Program was launched in 1980. The NFEC delivers literacy in one atoll a year through a network of volunteers identified by the atoll chief. The volunteers provide one-to-one instruction for a two-month period in basic reading, writing and mathematical skills. At the end of the tutorial period, the students take the literacy test. When the program was launched the literacy rate was estimated at 70 per cent. The one-atoll-a-year process is in progress and will be continued till the present adult literacy rate of 98.84 per cent reaches 100 per cent. Educational and awareness-raising programmes are broadcast by the Voice of Maldives and Television Maldives. There is hardly any difference between the number of male and female students from preschool to Grade X. However, the number of female students in post-secondary institutions is less than males. Even though there has been no comprehensive study or research done to find out the reasons for this gender disparity, certain contributing factors have been identified. The major factors, which contribute to gender disparity in enrollment in post-secondary institutions, are:

(i) Younger age of marriage for girls;
(ii) Motherhood at younger ages;
(iii) Lack of opportunities for secondary education in some island schools; and
(iv) Lower level of educational attainment of girls because they could not spend adequate time in schools.

Because of these factors, fewer girls meet the entrance requirement to enrol in tertiary institutions both in the Maldives and abroad in overseas universities and colleges. The student-teacher ratio declines as one progresses from lower grades to higher grades, the decline is particularly noticeable for the lower secondary level and even more at the higher secondary level. The fact that women in the Maldives are not able to achieve empowerment through higher education is shown in the low number of women among graduate teachers, although there is a fairly high number of non-graduate female teachers.

4

Discrimination Against Women

The explosive increase in numbers of young widows with children as a result of the Human Immunodeficiency Virus/ Acquired Immunodeficiency Syndrome (HIV/AIDS) pandemic and wars in these regions starkly exposed the critical link between denial of women's rights and extreme poverty. Personal status laws of women in the third world countries, continued to curtail women's rights entering into marriage, during marriage, or at the dissolution of marriage.

In Islamic states, the minimum age for marriage was eighteen for boys and seventeen for girls. If a woman over the age of seventeen married without the consent of a male guardian, the guardian could demand the annulment of the marriage if the husband was not of the same social standing as the wife, and as long as the wife was not pregnant. A man could legally have up to four wives simultaneously, while a woman could have only one husband.

Women did not have the same rights as men to end marriage: while the personal status law provided for the unilateral and unconditional right of a husband to effect divorce by repudiation, a woman seeking divorce was required to go to court and prove that her husband had neglected his marital duties. A serious consequence of limitations on women's equality in their private lives, such as whom to marry, was loss of citizenship for themselves and/or their children. Nationality laws in such disparate countries as Egypt, Sri Lanka, and Bangladesh denied women the right to transfer citizenship to their children. These laws, designed in part to curtail immigration and thus maintain the purity, loyalty, and cohesion of the nation, demonstrated the way in which discrimination on the bases of national origin and gender intersected to further entrench women's subordinate status in the family and in society. Despite years of protest and lawsuits by women's human rights groups, in May 2001 the State Consultative Council of Egypt dismissed the recent parliamentary plea to amend the 1975 Nationality Law.

Under this law, which contradicted the constitution, an Egyptian man could automatically transfer his nationality to his children while an Egyptian woman could do so only under limited circumstances: when the child was born in Egypt to a stateless father or to a father of unknown nationality, or when the child's relationship to his or her father could not be legally established.

The Egyptian Center for Women's Rights estimated that thousands of women married to foreigners and as many as one million children continued to suffer discrimination under this law. Working within this framework, the Maldives has carried a number of specific programmes, in the Gas of health services delivery, counseling, family planning and awareness raising, with special attention to maternal and child health. Increasing the participation of women in the process of development, both as participantsand beneficiaries, has also remained an important policy concern in the Maldives. A country wide institutional framework for undertaking programmes aimed at addressinggender issues is in place.

Women's Committees

Women's committees are well established at the communitylevel and enjoy a supportive relationship with the concerned Government authorities. Anational policy on women, incorporating a broad range of gender issues, is now beingfinalized. Further, the Government is working on new legislation that would ensuregreater protection and child care support for single mothers.

The Government is presently in the process of establishing a population coordination mechanism within the Ministry of Planning and National Development, with the responsibility to coordinate the planning and implementation of the national populationstrategy. This would ensure that population concerns are fully reflected in all relevantdevelopment programmes across sectoral boundaries.

Work on developing a clear andwide ranging population policy that addresses that diverse concerns of population anddevelopment are also underway.

The Maldives has made significant progress in achieving the goals of population and development. The wide dispersal of the population across the archipelago poses serious challenges in their quest for equitable,balanced and sustainable development.

Most importantly, the lack of scale economies increases the cost of providing basic services and imposes a heavy fiscal burden, on the Government Along with reproductive health concerns, Maldives is compelled to focus on linkagesbetween population environment. The uneven nature of population distribution andurban migration are some of the pressing issues in this regard. The capital of theMaldives, Male', is presently home to a quarter of the country's population. This has increased the demand for land and housing as well as for urban services and recreationfacilities.

To meet this demand the Government has embarked on the creation of settlements near Male'. This entails resettlement of uninhabited islands and the creation of new islands through reclamation of existing lagoons. At the same time, the Government also promotes regional development, with the objective of increasing income and employment opportunities, out side the capital region and revert the tide ofinternal migration. The Maldives currently allocates more than a quarter of the development budget on social development, of which education and health share asignificant part. Substantial investments are also being made in infrastructuredevelopment. However, additional resources are required in order to successfullyimplement population and development policies and achieve the objectives of nationaldevelopment.

The Committee on the Elimination of Discrimination against WomenTwenty-fourth session15 January-2 February 2001, the representative of Maldives informed there had been several positive developments since the submission of the initial report in 1998. The existing laws and policies did not discriminate against women in the areas of access to health services, education and employment, but socio-cultural factors restricted women's de facto enjoyment of rights in these areas.

Fifth Plan

Since the fifth National Development Plan period was almost over and the sixth National National Development Plan was currently being drawn up, the representative of the Maldives indicated that a separate section to reflect gender as a cross-cutting policy issue would be incorporated in the sixth National Development Plan to ensure that gender concerns are addressed in all development planning.

The representative indicated that measures, including public awareness-raising campaigns and promotion of family life education, had been taken to eliminate traditional stereotypical attitudes with regard to the roles of women, which were reinforced by images in textbooks and the media. The representative informed the Committee that although domestic violence was still largely considered to be a private matter, the Government had initiated public awareness campaigns to address such violence. Victims of domestic violence (women) could now report to the National Security Service, which dealt with the issue through the criminal law. Trafficking in women and girls was not considered to be a problem in Maldives, but with the growing expatriate population it was believed there would be a need to introduce anti-trafficking measures in the future. Prostitution was illegal and subject to strong religious and social sanctions, but it was thought to exist.

The Constitution indicated that the Head of State of Maldives should be Male, the political participation of women, as both voters and candidates, was encouraged. Despite public awareness and legal literacy campaigns aimed at increasing women's political participation, few women candidates presented themselves for election and only 10 per cent of the Majlis were women.

Women's Appointments

In 2000, two women had been appointed to the post of Assistant Island Chief, the second highest-ranking island official, while one woman had been appointed acting Atoll Chief. There were no legal barriers to women participating in the foreign service or in international organizations, but only one female diplomat was currently working abroad. There was no discrimination with regard to nationality and that women had equal rights with men to acquire, retain or change their nationality.

Marriage to a foreigner did not change a woman's nationality, and the 1998 Constitution had conferred Maldivian citizenship on children born to Maldivian mothers and foreign fathers. Women could obtain a passport and travel without the permission of their spouses or other male relatives. There was no disparity in the enrolment of girls and boys up to grade 10, which resulted in a very high rate of literacy among girls until secondary school. Only a limited number of students gained access to higher education because of the absence of a university in the country and transportation difficulties. There were no quotas for scholarships, including in traditionally male-dominated disciplines, such as engineering and law.

Although there was no discrimination between women and men where access to employment or remuneration were concerned, cultural practices promoted gender segregation in employment, with traditional views on the division of labour dictating that women's primary responsibility was with regard to childcare, the household and agricultural activities. The representative noted that women and men had equal access to health care and that the overall health situation had improved as a result of better access to health and medical services.

There was no disparity in the health status of girls and boys and no substantial difference in infant mortality and growth rates. A number of government initiatives had been introduced to address persisting disparities between the nutritional and health status of women and men during the reproductive years, and the media had launched public awareness campaigns on reproductive health.

Role of Majlis

A new Family Law had been enacted by the Majlis in December 2000 and would enter into force on 1 July 2001, which would include provisions on conditions for prenuptial agreements, polygamy and divorce. The new law would terminate the husband's right to non-judicial unilateral divorce and require court proceedings.

It would also provide for the equal division of joint property on divorce and financial provision from the former husband for children and former wives. Eighteen years would be established as the minimum legal age of marriage for both women and men, unless the marriage registrar determined that there were special circumstances, despite the fact that the sharia provided that an individual could enter into marriage upon puberty. In this regard, the Government had implemented a programme to discourage and prevent early marriages.

The Committee on discrimination against women commends the political will expressed in the Maldives "Vision 20/20" to work towards women's human rights as an integral dimension of national development. It welcomes the efforts at gender mainstreaming in the National Plan of Action and the National Development Plan. The recent measures taken to increase the participation of women as atoll chiefs and in island women's committees and atoll development committees. The Committee welcomes the progress achieved and reflected in a very high adult literacy rate for women, and parity among boys and girls in primary and secondary education. It commends the improved indicators on life expectancy for women and the ongoing efforts to bring the law on family relations into harmony with the Convention through the adoption of a new family law. The Committee commends the Government for amending its nationality law and for granting women equal rights with men to acquire, change or retain their nationality, and also to transfer their nationality to their children and the Government for the progressive development of the national machinery and the establishment in 1998 of a Ministry of Women's Affairs and Social Security.

The Committee is concerned with the reservations of article 7 (a) and 16 entered by the State party to the Convention. It is concerned that the reservation to article 7 (a) of the Convention on political participation supports the retention of legislative provisions excluding women from the office of the President and the Vice-President of the country. The Committee urges the Government to withdraw these reservations and to repeal legislation limiting women's political participation in public life.

The Committee regrets that there is an absence of an effective machinery to enforce the rights recognized by the Constitution and claim remedies. The Committee is also concerned that the constitutional provisions on fundamental rights do not include non-discrimination on the ground of sex. The Committee urges the Government to incorporate a provision against sex discrimination into the Constitution and to provide for the effective enforcement of fundamental rights.

The Committee notes with concern that early marriage and domestic responsibilities contribute to high dropout rates for girls. The Government to introduce minimum age of marriage laws and other programmes to prevent early marriage in line with the obligations of the Convention. The under- reporting of violence against women, including domestic violence and the absence of effective laws and law enforcement and a support system for women victims of violence. It is particularly concerned that violence against women is understood in the community and in the legal system as a private matter rather than as an infringement of human rights and a violation of the Convention. The Government to improve law enforcement measures, enact laws on violence against women, including domestic violence and marital rape, according to general recommendation on violence against women, and work with women's groups to obtain reliable data and provide relief to victims of violence. The Committee requests the Government to respond to this issue in national plans, based on the Beijing Platform for Action and the Commonwealth Plan of Action. It calls upon the Government to create public awareness on violence against women as an infringement of human rights that has grave social costs for the whole community.

Family Laws

The family laws discriminate against women and notes with concern the high divorce rates, which have an adverse impact on women and children. Government to enforce the new family law, which tries to address this problem, and to continue its efforts to reform all areas of family law so as to protect the human rights of women. The Government to obtain information on comparative jurisprudence seeking to interpret Islamic law in harmony with international human rights standards and the Beijing Platform for Action.

The health and nutrition of girls suffers after puberty and that maternal mortality and morbidity rates and the mortality rate of girls under age five remain at unsatisfactory levels. The

Committee is also concerned that patriarchal and stereotypical attitudes have a negative impact on women's health and nutrition. The Government to obtain information on the causes of maternal mortality, malnutrition and morbidity and the under-five mortality rate of girls, and to develop programmes to address those problems. The Committee on discrimination against women, requests the wide dissemination in the country of Maldives of the present concluding comments in order to make the people of Maldives, and particularly government administrators and politicians, aware of the steps that have been taken with regard to de jure and de facto equality for women and for the future steps.

In South Asia women take a back seat to men on everything from health care to education to legal protection, says a United Nations-sponsored report released recently. Women in South Asia may work from dawn to dusk, but their economic contribution is scarcely acknowledged at the national level and their access to health, education and other facilities lags far behind that of men, says the Human Development in South Asia report prepared annually by the Pakistan-based Human Development Centre. In the Maldives, girls are even 51% more likely to die before their fifth birthday than boys. During two days of meetings in Pakistan, including one with the army chief Gen Pervez Musharraf, Ms Sadiq said that the talk from the regime leadership was in favour of women's rights.

As a region South Asia has the lowest literacy rates and the largest gap between male and female literacy rates. Although South Asian women make up only 21 per cent of the world's female population, 44 per cent of the illiterate women in the world live in South Asia. Discrimination against South Asian women begins at, or even before, their birth, and follows them to their grave. In India 18 per cent more girls die before their fifth birthday than boys. In the Maldives girls are 51 per cent more likely to die before their fifth birthday than boys. Laws in most countries in South Asia favour men, deny women inheritance and marriage rights. In Afghanistan women can neither work nor attend school.

Women remain unable to gain equal access to inheritance or property and face other restrictions -- from purdah to so-called honour killings -- that effectively maintain their invisibility in society as a whole while subjecting them to terror and to violations of their basic human rights, says the watch report. The report warns that without women's participation no society can develop. The fact that South Asia lags so far behind in this area is a worrying sign that it will remain mired in poverty as the poorest, most illiterate and most malnourished in the world as well as the least gender-sensitive. Since it came to power in 1980, the Zimbabwe government had promised to enact land reform measures to redistribute to black Zimbabweans lands taken under white ownership during colonial rule, though without making significant progress before the end of 2000. In 2001, however, groups of ruling party supporters and reputed veterans of the war against colonial rule seized control of many white-owned farms by force in what the government described as a "spontaneous and popular uprising." Many black farmworkers, as well as white farmworkers and their families, were assaulted in the process. Some were killed. Many women on farms and in rural areas were raped or sexually assaulted with impunity.

In the U.S., the California State Legislature held hearings in January 2001 to address reports of continuing mental, physical, and sexual abuse, as well as medical neglect in the state's women's prisons. The hearings were prompted by the deaths of nine women at the Central California Women's Facility within a two-month period at the end of 2000. Legislators expressed concern over reports that some women inmates who requested medical attention prior to their deaths did not receive immediate attention. In one case, the cellmates of a deceased prisoner alleged that corrections officers had mocked the dying woman's pleas for assistance shortly before she died. There was particular concern that medical technical assistants (MTAs), prison guards with minimal medical training, were responsible for determining whether women inmates should see medical staff. More frequently, officials and medical doctors sought to convince the women to return to violent spouses in order to "save the family," and be "better wives."

NGOs in Uzbekistan attempted to provide hotlines and services to victims of domestic violence, but their resources were limited, and their services rarely reached beyond urban areas.

In 2001, UN-sponsored meetings addressed critical issues such as the gender dimensions of racism, gender-based persecution as grounds for asylum, and an international protocol on the collection of forensic evidence in cases of sexual violence. At the same time, the US and the European Union took steps on trafficking, international treaty ratification, funding for women's health, and trade that marginalised or ignored women's human rights. Women's rights activists found that many of these steps were tentative and inconsistent, and hoped that the international community's concern for women's rights in Afghanistan would be long-lasting and would result in stepped-up efforts to recognise women's human rights violations and curtail them also in other parts of the world.

Role of U.N.

The UN had an important follow-up role to play and it was hoped that the of Committee on the Elimination of All Forms of Discrimination against Women (CEDAW Committee) would develop a basis for governments to report regularly on their efforts to address the confluence of racism and sexism. The role of the CEDAW Committee expanded in 2001, as the Optional Protocol to the Convention on the Elimination of All Forms of Discrimination against Women came into force on December 22, 2000, enabling the committee to receive and consider complaints from individuals or groups within its jurisdiction.

Consequently, as part of the Global Consultations marking the fiftieth anniversary of the 1951 Convention Relating to the Status of Refugees, UNHCR convened a roundtable of experts to examine the issue of gender-based persecution and made recommendations on the interpretation of the refugee convention. Meanwhile, the World Health Organisation convened a group of forensic experts to begin drafting a standard protocol for the collection of evidence in cases of sexual violence.

In USA, the issue of women's rights did not feature visibly in any of Secretary of State Colin L. Powell's foreign visits but, to its credit, the Bush administration retained the position of senior coordinator for international women's issues, an office that in the past had played a critical role in the coordination and spearheading of women's human rights issues at the State Department. The Committee on the Elimination of Discrimination against Women this morning heard replies of Maldives to questions on its initial report, which was first considered on 24 January. At that time, the Committee's 23 experts asked questions regarding Maldives compliance with the Convention on the Elimination of All Forms of Discrimination against Women. A Committee was formed in order to identify the critical areas from the Beijing Platform of Action that had to be implemented in Maldives. These areas included education and training of women, women and health, violence against women, women and the economy, and women in power and decision-making.

The Deputy Minister said the prevalence of violence against women in Maldives was not known, due to a lack of research in that area. What transpired between a husband and wife and within the family was considered a private matter. Violence was perceived as a shameful issue and being a victim of violence brought disrespect to the family. There were many factors that contributed to the high divorce rate in Maldives, she said. One reason was the way in which a man could get a divorce. In the Islamic Sharia, the verbal pronouncement by the husband was adequate to terminate the marriage without having to go to court. Another reason for the high divorce rate was the lack of any social stigma on the divorced person. She said the situation of HIV/AIDS in Maldives was pretty good, so far. The people enjoyed relative freedom from the HIV/AIDS pandemic. The first case had been identified in 1991, and in the 10 years since, a total of 10 people had been infected with HIV/AIDS. Only one out of the 10 was a woman. As a precautionary measure to prevent the spread of the disease, expatriates who tested positive for the virus were returned to their country.

The Chairperson of the Committee, Charlotte Abaka of Ghana, said that unless democracy was based on respect for equality, it could not be called a democracy. It did not seem right that women were prohibited from being the President of the country just because the majority of the Constitutional Council had voted to retain that provision of the Constitution. Other issues that concerned the Committee included violence against women and the use of contraceptives.

Aneesa Ahmed, Deputy Minister of the Ministry of Women's Affairs and Social Security in Maldives, said two articles of the Constitution bar a woman from becoming either the President of the Republic or the Vice President. The question of removing the discriminatory clauses had been widely debated and a two-thirds majority of the Special Majlis, or the Constitutional Council, voted in favour of retaining the clauses.

In a democracy, the majority view had to be respected. However, this did not rule out the possibility of the people considering the matter in the next round of constitutional review. The courts of first instance in Maldives include the Criminal Court, the Civil Court, the Family Court, the Juvenile Court, and the Island Courts, she said. All cases of appeal were referred to the High Court. However, if a person was dissatisfied with the decision of the High Court, he or she may petition to the President, who is the highest authority of administering justice, to review the case. She said that although there was no separate Ombudsman's Office, the functions of the Ombudsman were carried out in various ways. If a person had grievances, he or she could petition a higher authority, such as a concerned minister or the President.

In cases of official malfeasance or the embezzlement of funds, people could take such cases to the Anti-Corruption Board. The national machinery for the advancement of women at present was comprised of the Gender Equality Council, the Ministry of Women's Affairs and Social Security and the Island and Ward Women's Committees, she said. A Gender Equality Council was established in December 2000, presided over by the President.

The Vice-Chairperson of the Council was the Minister of Women's Affairs and Social Security. The Council had members from all the Government Ministries and leading non-governmental organizations (NGOs), as well as most of the educational institutions under the College for Higher Education. For the initial report, she said information was first collected from the Island Women's Committees and Ward Women's Committee.

This was followed by consultations with those Committees and the National Women's Council. An independent consultant compiled the actual report. There was no direct involvement by NGOs. The phenomenon of NGOs acting as pressure groups was quite new in Maldives, and there were very few well-established ones. The objectives of the National Policy on Women were to incorporate women into the mainstream of economic activities and integrate their needs and perspectives in development planning. The Policy was also used to promote mass awareness on gender issues, among people at all levels.

Strategies for implementation of the Policy included strengthening the national machinery for women and undertaking massive advocacy, awareness and social mobilization programmes through mass media and women's organizations. A sectoral approach was used to address the problems of women in development in order to make them explicit within the framework of sector-based planning. Individual sectors such as health, education and media were entrusted with the responsibility of framing programmes and projects that consider women a distinct target group.

After the Beijing Conference on Women, the Ministry of Women's Affairs began formulating a National Plan of Action, she said. A Committee was formed, and it identified the critical areas from the Beijing Platform of Action that had to be implemented in Maldives. These areas included education and training of women, women and health, violence against women, women and the economy, and women in power and decision-making.

A seminar was then held, and officials from all Government Ministries and representatives from all sectors of civil society finalized the draft Plan of Action. It has since been submitted to the Government for endorsement. The Deputy Minister said that there had been no temporary special measures taken to improve the position of women. There were no quotas for the cabinet, the People's Majlis or any leadership position in the atolls or islands.

The use of quotas had not been contemplated for awarding scholarships or fellowships in higher education or vocational training. Nevertheless, introducing quotas had been recommended to the Government as a strategic action to achieve a society where women and men were equal in the political, social and economic spheres. The prevalence of violence against women in Maldives was not known due to a lack of research in that area, she said. What transpired between a husband and wife and within the family should not be made public. Women hesitated to report domestic violence. Violence was perceived as a shameful issue and being a victim of violence brought shame and disrespect to the family. As there was no alternative housing facility for the victims of domestic violence, women often had no choice but to return to living in the same house. In response to the question on whether the mother could have her child on her passport without the father's consent, she said with regret that this was not the case.

Statistics revealed that there had been a sharp decline in women's participation in the labour force since the late 1970s, she said. No studies had been done on how this had affected women's lives so there was no empirical evidence of increased poverty among women. On a positive note, in recent years there had been a slow but steady rise in the number of young women who sought employment in the tourism sector.

Permanent methods such as tubal ligation and vasectomy were also available at hospitals. Condoms, oral pills, injection, and IUDs were accessible through the Island Health Posts, Health Centres, Family Planning Clinics and the Society for Health Education, an NGO.

Prescriptions were not required for obtaining contraceptives unless a health worker found it necessary to refer a woman to a doctor in order to have her general health assessed prior to recommending her oral contraceptives. Once a couple was registered for family planning services, either spouse could obtain contraceptives. All marriages in the Maldives must be conducted in accordance with the Family Law, she said.

Age for Marriage

The minimum legal age for marriage was recently raised to 18 years. There was no restriction on marriage between Maldivians and migrants. Marriage to a Maldivian provides the foreign national certain benefits such as automatic resident visa and the waving of the resident permit fee. There were many factors that contributed to the high divorce rate in Maldives, she said. One reason was the way in which a man could get a divorce.

In the Islamic Sharia, the verbal pronouncement by the husband was adequate to terminate the marriage without having to go to court. Reporting to the courts was required only for the purpose of registering the divorce. Another reason for the high divorce rate was the lack of any social stigma on the divorced person. Remarriage among the same couple who were once divorced was also fairly common.

The Fourth World Conference on Women defined "Women and Health" as one critical area of concern in the Platform for Action and established five strategic objectives. In doing so, it emphasized the importance of a holistic and life-cycle approach to women's health. The objectives are:

– increase women's access throughout the life cycle to appropriate, affordable and quality health care, information and related services;
– strengthen preventive programmes that promote women's health;
– undertake gender-sensitive initiatives that address sexually transmitted diseases, HIV/AIDS, and sexual and reproductive health issues;
– promote research and disseminate information on women's health;
– increase resources, and monitor follow-up for women's health.

The Platform also addressed, a number of specific health causes, such as mental health, cancer, occupational health, disability issues, tropical diseases and suggested to "increase financial and other support from all sources for preventive, appropriate biomedical, behavioral, epidemiological and health service research on women's health issues and for research on the social, economic and political causes of women's health problems, and their consequences, including the impact of gender and age inequalities, especially with respect to chronic and non-communicable diseases, particularly cardiovascular diseases and conditions, cancers, reproductive tract infections and injuries, HIV/AIDS and other sexually transmitted diseases, domestic violence, occupational health, disabilities, environmentally related health problems, tropical diseases and health aspects of ageing". The people in Maldives, enjoyed relative freedom from the HIV pandemic. The first HIV case was identified in 1991 and in the 10 years since, a total of 10 people had been infected with HIV/AIDS. Only one out of the 10 was a woman. As a precautionary measure to prevent the spread of HIV/AIDS, expatriates who were tested positive for the virus were returned to their country.

5

Women's Participation in Government

The Republic of the Maldives is a 750 km long archipelago. However, less than 300 islands are actually inhabited, and many of these islands (72) are held by tourist companies on leases from the Government of the Maldives. These are known as tourist resorts.

The population growth rate in the Maldives is one of the highest in South Asia: 2.75 percent per annum. It is expected to double in the next few years. Such increases would be due to a dramatic drop in mortality rates, without a corresponding decline in fertility (the birth rate is high at 46 per 1,000). The problems caused by the rapid population growth are compounded by the small amount of arable land available in the country. There is the additional problem of environmental degradation as evidenced by the loss of vegetation, diminishing supplies of firewood and drinking water and deforestation. The government has yet to develop a comprehensive national population policy and programme. Malé is the capital of the Republic, and had 62,973 inhabitants, thereby accounting for roughly 25 per cent of the population of the country.

The density of population in Malé is very high, but for the country as a whole, population is scattered in over 200 islands (excluding 72 industrial and tourist islands where the Maldivians can stay as long as they are employed but cannot live on a permanent basis). The fact that commutation facilities between islands are not highly developed, and furthermore that commuting by air between distant islands is relatively expensive, have led to the development of a fragmented labour market.

Labour Market

The demand for labour in one island cannot be easily met by supply from another island. Adverse weather conditions, the relatively high cost of travelling by motorised boats and the abundance of coral reefs are factors which impede labour mobility and have seriously affected the development of a unified national labour market. On an average, out of 2 marriages, one marriage ends up in divorce. It is therefore not uncommon for women to marry and re-marry several times during their reproductive years. As a result, the birth rate tends to be very high in the Maldives. It is therefore to be expected that the average annual net addition to the workforce, based on the population growth trends, would be high in the Maldives.

Despite such problems, the Maldives economy has been growing rapidly since 1981. In the 1980s real GDP grew by 11.1 percent per annum while the annual rate of growth in real GDP per capita was just about 8 percent. Much of the growth, however, has been concentrated on Malé, the capital of the country and in the surrounding Malé atoll. In the 1990s, the GDP growth rate moderated, and since 1993, the GDP has been growing at an average annual rate of 6.5 percent. High growth rates in GDP for over 15 years have made it possible for the Maldivians to have the highest per capita income (US $1,200 in 1996) among the SAARC countries. The economic prosperity, however, is concentrated on the Malé atoll, which is the hub of trade and commerce and tourism in the country. High growth rates in the 1980s and the early 1990s led to problems of current account deficits (CAD) and inflation.

By 1995 the fiscal deficit was running around 21 percent, and inflation was in double-digit. Under pressure from the IMF, the government of the Maldives was forced to adopt macro-economic stabilisation programmes. Inflation is now down to 5 percent per annum, and the fiscal deficit has also been brought to manageable limits.

An exhaustive study has been made by the World Bank regarding the need for education and skills development in the Maldives and had this to state:

Education and skills development are critical to any country, but perhaps especially so in the Republic of Maldives, with its rapidly growing population, fragile eco-system, and limited range of economic opportunities. The Maldivian population is very young - close to a third of the population is in school - and demand for education is strong and rising. At the same time, skill shortages are pervasive throughout the economy. Large numbers of expatriates have been employed temporarily to meet these gaps. In fact Maldives need to focus on education to sustain the expansion of its fisheries and sustain the expansion of its tourism - based economy, to develop alternative sources of employment, to begin the handover of skilled posts from expatriates to national citizens and to create the awareness needed to slow population growth in all the islands.

The potential labour force of a country is the number of people (both sexes) in the age group of 15-64. Many of these people may not be actively looking for jobs (e.g. housewives and students in full time education). In many developing countries, however, children below the age of 15 participate in the workforce in various on-farm and off-farm activities. The actual labour force may therefore be greater or smaller than the potential labour force. We have to depend upon the earlier 1990 Census figures. According to the 1990 Census, only 49.5 percent of the Maldivians aged 15 years or above were economically active. Assuming that very few of the older people above the age of 64 actually participate in the labour market, the labour force participation rate was low in the Maldives, as compared with other South Asian countries. When compared with developed countries the labour force participation rate in the Maldives is very low: for example, the rate is 63.5 percent in Australia, which is comparable to other OECD countries.

In this connection, a number of considerations emerge from the Population and Housing Census of Maldives. First, an important conclusion is that the labour force participation rate (49.5 percent) in the Maldives is lower than in many developing countries such as Sri Lanka, Mauritius and French Polynesia, but the Maldivian figure is comparable to other Islamic countries of the region such as Pakistan (49.3 per capita) and Bangladesh (50.3 percent). An explanation for such phenomenon is to be sought in two different ways: (1) Because of continuing high fertility, the percentage of population below the age of 15 is very high.

Work-force

Such young population is automatically excluded from the definition of the labour force used in the Population and Housing Census of Maldives, although many of these young people are possibly engaged in part, or full-time economic activity, especially in the fisheries sector. (2) Again, in many Islamic countries such as Pakistan and Bangladesh women do not traditionally participate in the workforce but generally perform household chores. Labour force participation by females in the Maldives was only 20.2 percent as compared with 43.3 percent in Mauritius; and 48.5 percent in French Polynesia. With an actual workforce of 55,544 in employment, the Maldives achieved near full employment by 1990, when the unemployment rate for the economy as a whole was reported to be only 0.8 percent. Thus the unemployment figures emerging from the Census of 1990 may have underestimated the problem, because of the definitions used.

Several persons, particularly women, who were principally engaged in household activity were defined as economically inactive, but not unemployed. Such definition could be misleading, because a significant percentage of economically inactive population might have withdrawn from the labour force because of unavailability of jobs in their home atolls, which were located far away from Malé and the Malé atoll. Secondly, unemployment figures are also likely to be understated because of under-employment, which is likely to be widely prevalent in the Maldives. In the fishery sector of the Maldives, it is possible that many men, particularly older men are formally employed but have been reduced to the status of marginal workers. Third, the reluctance, no doubt due to social and cultural factors, of Maldivian men and women to accept menial and inferior jobs, particularly in the tourist resorts has led to a very tight labour market situation in the hospitality industries, thereby making it necessary for the expatriate labour from

Bangladesh and Sri Lanka to fill up the job vacancies in

the relatively unskilled sectors of the labour market. As a result, there are about 22,500 expatriates working in the Maldives. We shall of course examine later the problems associated with the presence of a large expatriate workforce in the Maldives.

Occupational Shift

During the period of rapid economic growth in the 1980s and the early 1990s there had been a major occupational shift in the Maldives. Traditionally, the primary sector comprising agriculture, fisheries and coral and sand mining was the main contributor to GDP. In 1977, 45.0 percent of the employed workforce was in the fishery sector. But it declined to 20.6 percent by 1990.

A major reason for this decline was no doubt the adoption of new technology such as motorised fishing boats (Masdhonis) for deep sea or pelagic fishing. Moreover, many women who were earlier employed in the fishery sector, mainly on the job of drying fish for export to Sri Lanka. The emergence of a market for frozen fish and canned fish has now led to a relative decline in the importance of dry fishing. Canned fish is exported to the distant markets of Europe, whereas frozen fish goes to Thailand and other Asian countries.

The shift in the fish exports market led to a sharp decline in demand for the services of women, who withdrew from the labour market in the absence of other alternative jobs in their own rural atolls. It is also possible that the attraction of higher paying jobs in Malé and the Malé atoll resulted in the migration of workers, especially men, away from the rural atolls. The occupational shift in the 1980s was also brought about by the spectacular growth of the tourism sector in the 1980s.

Such rapid growth of tourism led to a spurt in construction activity of resorts and hotels, and subsequently a substantial increase in demand for workers in the service sector. Many of the jobs created in the service and construction sector were not suitable for Maldivians either because these needed special skills or because these involved unskilled menial work for which the Maldivians feel no attraction. Thus the gap created between demand and supply was filled up by the expatriates.

The booming Maldivian economy in the 1980s led to a paradoxical labour market situation. The Maldivian women withdrew from the labour markets in the rural atolls, because of the shift in the export market of fish and the decline in the importance of dry fishing. But these women did not go for jobs, which were now available in the booming tourist sector - in holiday resorts, hotels and guest houses, and in construction and trade.

Public Sector

Rapid growth of employment in the public sector between 1985 and 1994, however, created new job opportunities for women, The percentage of women employed in the government sector was only 22 percent in 1985, but this increased to 29 percent in 1994, whilst the total number of jobs in the government sector increased from 8,836 to 18,060, i.e. an increase of 104 percent.

Women are still in relatively junior government jobs, but their number in senior positions has been rising in more recent years. An interesting aspect of employment in the Maldives is the high proportion of the workforce who are employed on the "own-account".

In other words, these people are either self-employed or are employed on a sub-contract basis. The Census recorded 41.8 percent of the local workforce as "own-account" workers, whereas 45.2 percent were employees, and the remainder were employers (2.8 percent), family workers (4.5 percent), or did not state their employment status (5.7 percent).

"Own-account" workers dominate agriculture, forestry and fishing. But they are also important in "manufacturing", suggesting that there are few large employers but many small businesses dominating the manufacturing sector in the Maldives. Working on 'own-account' has been sharply declining since 1977, when 85 percent of the entire workforce (aged 15 years and over) was measured as working on 'own-account'. As stated earlier, expatriate employment comprises nearly 28 percent of the total workforce in the Maldives: Sri Lanka accounts for 49 percent of all expatriate employment, Bangladesh. The bulk of expatriates were employed in the private sector, the remainder (17.6 percent) were employed in the government sector, public sector enterprises and development projects.

Tourist Industry

Many of the expatriate workers were employed in tourism and tourism-related activities, because of their special skills such as managers, accountants, chefs, engineers, machine operators, etc. But very large numbers were also employed in unskilled occupations such as labourers, peons, domestic servants, and so on.

Such rapid growth of the expatriate population, particularly in unskilled jobs, might lead to social tensions in a relatively homogeneous society like the Maldives. Unskilled expatriate workers tend to resent the manner in which they are treated by their employers and by the Maldives Government. First, they have to spend in the range of US $500 on the various services provided by the local recruiting agent in India, Bangladesh and Sri Lanka to get jobs in the Maldives.

Most of these unskilled workers have to heavily borrow from their relatives, or mortgage and sell their farming land to raise such funds to be able to secure a job in the Maldives. Although the workers have their initial investments reimbursed by most employers at the end of their probation period, which may last up to 6 months, they have no security of stay, as they get only a year's renewable contract, and one year's visa to live in the Maldives. The working visa is seldom extended beyond 2 years, and the workers are forced to return home after the initial 2 year period.

Labour Legislation

There is still no comprehensive labour legislation in the Maldives to protect workers from the exploitation of their employers, although a legislation is now being drafted and hopefully will be put in place soon. Monthly wages for unskilled expatriate workers vary between US$100 and US$150, but in the very high cost Maldivian economy, such wages do not allow for comfortable living. In any case, workers have to save to make remittances to their poor relatives at home, thereby forcing them into a low standard living, which few Maldivians would be willingly to accept. Employers provide free accommodation, but as many as 12 workers have to share one room and common facilities. Senior executives and top managers, who are mostly recruited from

Europe, the USA and Canada, are generously treated, have luxury apartments, and can earn as much as US $3,000 per month.

It would appear that a number of policy measures involving institutional reforms would be needed to overcome some of the major bottlenecks in the labour market of the Maldives.

Some of these are listed below:

(1) A major aspect of the Maldivian labour market is its fragmented character. This is largely because of the geophysical characteristics of the country. The Malé atoll is relatively overdeveloped, and has most of the educational and infrastructure facilities. Shortages of labour are acutely fel. in Malé and the Malé atoll, and in the resort islands. But surplus workers especially women in the rural atolls, cannot move to seize the job opportunities elsewhere because of cultural, geographical and family reasons. Most Maldivians live in about 200 islands, but 90 percent of islands have less than 1,000 inhabitants. The people live in widely scattered islands in small groups, and cannot therefore enjoy developed commutation facilities between islands. Improvement in ferry services between islands is a pre-requisite for better distribution of labour geographically. Private operators are unlikely to provide improved ferry services without guaranteed project. Public sector intervention is therefore unavoidable.

(2) An acnte problem in the labour market is the gradual decline of the unorganised sector in which most 'own-account' workers are employed. As the growth of the Maldivian economy continues in the future, there will be an increasing demand for labour from the organised sector. The unemployment in the unorganised sector may not lead to a situation in which unemployed workers from this sector would seek employment in the modern sectors of the economy. The lack of 'automatic adjustments' in the various sectors of the labour market might lead to a further influx of foreign workers into the Maldives. Suitable institutions for creating jobs in the unorganised sector should be a high priority of the

Maldives Government. These institutions should aim at providing credit facilities for new cottage industries in the remote islands.

(3) It seems that a significant percentage of workers in the traditional sectors such as the fisheries sector are underemployed, or are actually "marginal" workers. Institutional reforms are needed to provide underemployed marginal labourers with opportunities for productive employment to ease the shortage of supply of labour. For example, women workers who are now underemployed (if not unemployed) can be given alternative jobs in export-oriented tuna canning facilities. It may be interesting to note that when the world prices for frozen tuna recently collapsed, and a Japanese partner withdrew from a new joint cannery venture with the Government of Maldives, the government did not abandon the project. This project, despite some opposition from World Bank, continued, and efforts were made to integrate the modernisation of a cannery with the development facility for frozen tuna. This decision gave the industry flexibility. The Maldives now has a modern tuna canning complex designed and run to high international standards, producing top quality products for sale under international brand labels.

The cannery complex in the Maldives employs very few Maldivians, and is largely run by expatriate workers, especially from Sri Lanka. Government intervention is needed for providing suitable incentives to Maldivian women to seek employment in the modernised fishery sector.

(4) It is necessary to highlight once again the low participation rate of women in the workforce in Maldives. Early marriages, high birth rates and high rates of divorce do not create a conducive environment for work for women, who spend most of their lives in child-bearing, or child-rearing. Although there is no clear evidence of widespread violence against women, the Maldivian women occupy an inferior status in the household. Lack of economic independence accounts for women's inferiority.

Economic Independence

In more recent years, women have sought to achieve economic independence by joining the workforce in the public sector mostly in inferior, or junior positions. But the cultural factors still prevent women from taking up jobs in the booming tourist sector and hospitality industries. Fortunately, however, the Maldivian Government is aware of the need for greater participation by women in the workforce. A Ministry of Women's Affairs and Social Welfare was recently established in order to follow the SAARC plan for development of women. Island committees dealing with women's welfare have been established with funding from the United Nations. There are at present women's centres on islands, which are dedicated to women's affairs, in particular to give women a sense of self-confidence.Such institutional reforms are in the right direction, but much more efforts are to be directed to attract women to join the workforce.

(5) The World Bank report on the Maldives pointed out the difficulty in attracting workers away from their home islands "where 'affluent subsistence' has provided an attractive traditional way of life". Hence Maldivian workers hate to do menial work which is associated in their perceptions with human degradation. When they do such jobs, they do it with a purpose (such as achieving a definite savings target), and leave their jobs when that purpose is fulfilled. Hence, of course, the labour turn-over rate is very high in the Maldives.

At the same time, the educational facilities in the Maldives are relatively underdeveloped and do not provide adequate opportunities for development of skills for highly skilled jobs. Until 1953 secular education was banned in the Maldives. Facilities for religious education did exist, but English-medium education started only in 1962. Education began to spread only after 1978, and many new schools were then established. Yet the focus of education today continues to be theoretical rather than practical and vocational training.

Post-secondary education facilities are still very inadequate. There are at present only five post-secondary institutions, or centres in the Maldives. These are:

(i) Institute of Health Sciences
(ii) Institute of Teacher Education

(iii) Institute of Hotel and Catering Services
(iv) Maldives Institute of Technical Education and
(v) Maldives Centre for Management and Administration.

Of these five institutions, only the last two are directly under the Ministry of Planning, Human Resources and Environment and provide for multi-sectoral training.

The post-secondary education facilities in the Maldives are totally inadequate to give places to about 1,700 students who complete secondary education every year. Many Maldivians have therefore to go overseas for higher education. There are currently about 110 scholarships for overseas training, and 200 places every year are available at post-secondary institutes in the Maldives. There is therefore a wide gap between the availability of higher education facilities and the demand for places. Without better and more broad-based educational facilities, the dependence of the Maldives on expatriate workers for skilled jobs would likely continue. The Third 3-Year Plan in the Maldives has now identified the need for a University, but University education in itself would not solve the kind of bottlenecks in the labour market now being experienced in the Maldives. A radical re-thinking of the entire institutional structure of the current educational system in the Maldives is urgently called for.

(6) The World Bank, pointed out that the low level of educational attainment of the national workforce has contributed to the employment of under-qualified personnel in Government, where in the past, all post-primary school leavers were bonded to serve a minimum period. The growth of the public sector employment from about 10,000 in 1988 to about 20,000 in 1996 would suggest a tendency towards overstaffing. Many of these public sector employees are to be retrained for private sector jobs. Although major strides have already been made in improving access to primary and lower secondary schools, there are still significant shortfalls in upper secondary and post-secondary facilities. Rapid growth of the school-age population would continue to place more demand on post-secondary education.

Expansion and improvement of post-secondary educational facilities would require urgent attention in order to train the Maldivians for the skilled jobs in the private sector and to reduce the dependence upon expatriate workers. The case for an urgent institutional reform of the educational sector does appear to have an overwhelming importance. Surplus staff in the public sector could be released for employment in labour shortage industries, such as tourism.

The institutional responses needed for the current main problems of the labour market in the Maldives are easily identifiable. As long as economic growth remains dependent upon tourism and upon the supply of both skilled and unskilled foreign workers, a steady long-term growth of the economy cannot be taken for granted. The key is to have a domestic labour market in which demand for and supply of labour are generally adjusted internally.

On the demand side annual economic growth rates of 6 to 10 percent would ensure an escalating demand for labour in the growth sectors of the economy. Despite full employment in the Maldives, there is a pool of untapped supply of labour if the female participation rate in the labour force could be increased through institutional measures, such as providing adequate child-care centres for women with young children, and offering suitable work environment for women. In Islamic countries, like the Maldives, women are generally shy of a work environment in which they are not relatively segregated from male workers.

(7) The difficulty in labour adjustment is partly caused by geographical dispersion of the islands, and partly by the lack of skills of the workforce released from the dwindling traditional sector for jobs in the modern growth sectors. Suitable manpower planning, coupled with the provision of adequate vocational and professional training facilities should solve the problem of low skills. However, the enormous costs of higher education would possibly call for funding assistance from other SAARC and developed countries. It is not likely that the cultural factors that discourage women from working on tourist resorts would be overcome easily. So, the dependence on unskilled workers from SAARC countries such as Bangladesh and Sri Lanka would continue in the foreseeable future, but conditions for work for such workers would have to be both controlled and improved by governmental intervention to prevent any large scale

discontent among foreign workers.

(8) Geographical dispersion also creates other formidable problems for the Maldivian economy. There is now an overwhelming case for more balanced economic growth - away from Malé. The Malé atoll already suffers from excessive crowding and development. As a result, there is an extreme shortage of housing in Malé, thereby causing very high property prices and scarcities of rental accommodation. Government policy has to be directed to a more balanced development of other atolls, so that these can function as self-contained development centres within the national economy. The Maldivian Government has already identified one island each in eight atolls as regional centres which would develop into 'growth poles' to provide new economic opportunities and services. Success of policy will be judged by the performance of these growth centres.

6

National Policy

South Asia enters the 21st century with 515 million people in absolute poverty, about 400 million illiterate adults, and almost 80 million malnourished children. Preventable diseases kill 3.2 million children each year. Girls and women form the vast majority of these deprived millions. The balance sheet of the region must be put in proper perspective to objectively assess the real successes and failures in the context of the last 50 years. The economic growth in South Asia has increased significantly during the last half century. The gross domestic product (GDP) per capita has almost tripled since 1960. All three major sectors—agriculture, industry and service—have witnessed reasonable growth rates over the last 30-35 years.

The contribution of agriculture to GDP has decreased steadily over time, as primary product prices have gone down in world markets. At the same time, the industrial and service sectors have become more important contributors to the economy. The trend towards increasing industrialisation has been largely responsible for improved growth rates and has been matched by an increase in employment opportunities.

Increased female employment has also been witnessed in all countries of South Asia. Significant productivity gains accompanied these structural trans-formations. Across the board, there have been improvements in output per worker, including in agriculture. Industrial value added per worker also increased significantly, particularly in Sri Lanka and India. South Asia is diversifying rapidly into markets such as computer software. Bangalore, for example, is one of the world's largest software production centres. These markets and others like them are driven by new and innovative entrepreneurial initiative. However, just as critical have been the expanding middle classes that create the appropriate consumer market for these new sectors to emerge. This is perhaps the largest single positive impact of South Asia's economic development in the post-war era.

Human Rights

In Maldives, the Government generally respected the human rights of its citizens in a number of areas; however, its record was poor in some other areas, particularly with regard to political and religious freedoms. The President's power to appoint a significant portion of the Parliament constrains citizens' ability to change their government.

The Government limits freedom of assembly and association. There are significant restrictions on the freedom of religion; in the past, the Government has detained arbitrarily and expelled foreigners for proselytising and detained citizens who converted. Although the Government has undertaken a number of programs addressing women's issues, women face a variety of legal and social disadvantages.

The Government also restricts worker rights. Nonetheless, in recent years there has been some progress in certain areas. The Majlis has assumed a more active political role in recent years, and its members routinely differ with government policy on many issues. The courts were reorganised in 1997, and a new Constitution, which provides for the protection of certain fundamental rights, went into effect at the beginning of 1998. In addition procedural rules limiting indefinite police detention were instituted in 1998, and the presidential nominating process involved competition among candidates for the first time in 1998. A continued easing of government restrictions and the Press Council's balanced handling of issues related to journalistic standards allowed a greater diversity of views in the media, although most media outlets are controlled by persons friendly to the Government or by the Government itself.

There were no reports of beatings or any other mistreatment of persons in police custody during the year; however, convicted criminals may be flogged under judicial supervision when this punishment is prescribed by Islamic law as interpreted in the country (i.e., only when the criminal confesses to the crime and only for the offences of marital infidelity and alcohol abuse). There were no public floggings during the year.

In 1998 there were two private floggings (carried out without public spectators) due to the confession of an extramarital affair. The man was subsequently banished, and the woman was placed under house arrest for 12 months. Punishments usually are confined to fines, compensatory payment, house arrest, imprisonment, or banishment to a remote atoll. The Government generally permits those who are banished to receive visits by family members. The country's prison was destroyed by fire in 1999. Children also are housed in separate centre for juveniles. Prison conditions at the current facility, including food and housing, generally are adequate. Prisoners are allowed to work in prison and given the opportunity for regular exercise and recreation. Spouses are allowed privacy during visits with incarcerated partners. However, Amnesty International (AI) reported that in 1998, in the since-destroyed prison, prisoners were mistreated. The Government is surveying prison facilities in other countries to incorporate international standards and improvements in the reconstruction of the prison, and it has requested training for prison guards.

The 1997 Constitution states that no person shall be arrested or detained for more than 24 hours without being informed of the grounds for arrest or detention; however, in 1998 authorities arbitrarily detained foreign Christians for allegedly proselytising and detained citizens who supposedly converted.

Police initiate investigations based on suspicion of criminal activity or in response to written complaints from citizens, police officers, or government officials. They are not required to obtain warrants for arrests. Based on the results of police investigations, the Attorney General refers cases to the appropriate court. The authorities generally keep the details of a case confidential until they are confident that the charges are likely to be upheld.

Depending upon the charges, a suspect may remain free, be detained in prison, or placed under house arrest for 15 days during investigations. The President may extend pretrial detention for an additional 30 days, but in most cases the suspect is released if not brought to trial within 15 days. Those who are released pending trial may not leave a specific atoll. The law providing for the indefinite detention of individuals under investigation was revised substantially in 1998. Within 24 hours of an arrest, an individual must be told of the grounds for the arrest. An individual can then be held for 7 days. If no legal proceedings have been initiated within 7 days, the case is referred to an anonymous three-member civilian commission appointed by the President that can authorise an additional 15 days' detention. After that time, if legal proceedings still have not been initiated, a judge must sanction the continued detention on a monthly basis. There is no right to legal counsel during police interrogation. There is no provision for bail.

The Government may prohibit access to a telephone and nonfamily visits to those under house arrest. While there have been no reported cases of incommunicado detention in recent years, the law does not provide safeguards against this abuse. There were no reports of the external exile of citizens, although 24 foreigners suspected of proselytisation were banished for life in 1998. The Government sometimes banishes convicted criminals to inhabited atolls away from their home communities; a man who confessed to an extramarital affair in April 1998 was banished for 1 year. AI reported that in 1999, 10 persons from Faafu Magoodhoo were banished, reportedly without trial, for trying to organise a demonstration against the local atoll chief. The 1997 Constitution does not provide for an independent judiciary, and the judiciary is subject to executive influence. In addition to his authority to review High Court decisions, the President influences the judiciary through his power to appoint and dismiss judges, all of whom serve at his pleasure and are not subject to confirmation by the Majlis. The President nevertheless has removed only two judges since 1987. Both dismissals followed the recommendation of the Justice Ministry that found the judges' professional qualifications to be below standard. The President may also grant pardons and amnesties. In September 1997, the court system, under the Ministry of Justice, was reorganised and court administration has improved. There are three courts: One for civil matters; one for criminal cases; and one for family and juvenile issues.

High Court in Male

On the recommendation of the Ministry of Justice, the President appoints a principal judge for each court. There is also a High Court on Male, which is independent of the Justice Ministry and which handles a wide range of cases, including politically sensitive ones. The High Court also acts as court of appeals. Under a 1995 presidential decree, High Court rulings can be reviewed by a five-member advisory council appointed by the President. The President also has authority to affirm judgments of the High Court, to order a second hearing, or to overturn the Court's decision.

In addition to the Male courts, there are 204 general courts on the islands. There are no jury trials. Most trials are public and are conducted by judges and magistrates trained in Islamic, civil, and criminal law. Magistrates usually adjudicate cases on outer islands, but when more complex legal questions are involved, the Justice Ministry will send more experienced judges to handle the case. The Constitution provides that an accused person be presumed innocent until proven guilty, and that an accused person has the right to defend himself "in accordance with Shari'a" (Islamic law). During a trial, the accused also may call witnesses, and be assisted by a lawyer. Courts do not provide lawyers to indigent defendants. Judges question the concerned parties and attempt to establish the facts of a case. Civil law is subordinate to *Shari'a,* which is applied in situations not covered by civil law as well as in certain acts such as divorce and adultery. Courts adjudicating matrimonial and criminal cases generally do not allow legal counsel in court because, according to a local interpretation of Shari'a, all answers and submissions should come directly from the parties involved.

However, the High Court allows legal counsel in all cases, including those in which the right to counsel was denied in the lower court. Under the country's Islamic practice, the testimony of two women is required to equal that of one man in matters involving Shari'a, such as adultery, finance, and inheritance. In other cases, the testimony of men and women are equal. The 1997 Constitution prohibits security officials from opening or reading letters, telegrams, and wireless messages or monitoring telephone conversations, "except as expressly provided by law."

The NSS may open the mail of private citizens and monitor telephone conversations if authorised in the course of a criminal investigation. Although the 1997 Constitution provides residential premises and dwellings should be inviolable, there is no legal requirement for search or arrest warrants. The Attorney General or a commanding officer of the police must approve the search of private residences. The Government is attempting to concentrate the population on the larger islands by providing government services and concentrating job creation efforts there. The smaller islands are to be provided with only "basic services." However, no one is being coerced to move to the larger islands under this program.

The Penal Code prohibits inciting citizens against the Government. However, a 1990 amendment to the Penal Code decriminalised "any true account of any act of commission or omission past or present by the Government in a lawfully registered newspaper or magazine, so as to reveal dissatisfaction or to effect its reform." Regulations that make publishers responsible for the content of the material they published remain in effect but did not result in any legal actions during the year. Most major media outlets are owned either by the Government or its sympathisers. Nonetheless these sympathetic outlets do on occasion strongly criticise the Government.

Press Council

The Press Council is composed of lawyers, private and government media representatives, and other government officials. The Council reviews charges of journalist misconduct (advising the Ministry of Information, Arts, and Culture on measures to be taken against reporters, when appropriate) and promotes professional standards within the media (recommending reforms and making suggestions for improvement). Private journalists have said that they are satisfied with the Council's objectivity and performance. The Government agreed that private journalists, rather than the Government, should take responsibility for preparation of a journalistic code of ethics. Individual newspapers and journals established their own ethical guidelines in many cases.

There were no reports of government censorship of the electronic media, nor were there closures of any publications or reports of intimidation of journalists. Television news and public affairs programming routinely discussed topics of current concern and freely criticised government performance. Regular press conferences with government ministers instituted in 1995 continued. Journalists are more self-confident than in the past; self-censorship appears to have diminished, although it remains a problem.

In 1997 the Government banned a book written by an elderly close relative of the President for its derogatory comments about a deceased previous president, after the relatives of the latter complained.

Although 88 newspapers and periodicals are registered with the Government, only about 60 regularly publish. Aafathis, a morning daily, is often critical of government policy. Another daily, Miadhu, began publishing in 1996, and Haveeru is the evening daily. Both Miadhu's and Haveeru's publishers are pro-government.

The Government owns and operates the only television and radio station. It does not interfere with foreign broadcasts or with the sale of satellite receivers. Reports drawn from foreign newscasts are aired on the Government television station. Cable News Network (CNN) is shown, uncensored, daily on local television. In 1996 a company began providing internet service. The Government enacted no regulations governing internet access but blocks distribution of pornographic material via the internet. There are no legal prohibitions on the import of foreign publications except for those containing pornography or material otherwise deemed objectionable to Islamic values. No seizures of foreign publications were reported during the year. There are no reported restrictions on academic freedom. Some teachers reportedly are vocal in their criticism of the Government on some issues.

The Constitution

The 1997 Constitution provides for freedom of assembly "peaceably and in a manner that does not contravene the law;"

however, the Government imposes limits on this right in practice. The Home Ministry permits public political meetings during electoral campaigns but limits them to small gatherings on private premises. The Government registers clubs and other private associations if they do not contravene Islamic or civil law; however, the Government imposes some limits on freedom of association.

While not forbidden by law, the President officially discourages political parties on the grounds that they are inappropriate to the homogeneous nature of society. However, many Majlis members were active and outspoken critics of the Government and have stimulated closer parliamentary examination of government policy. The 1997 Constitution designates Islam as the official state religion, and the Government interprets this provision to impose a requirement that citizens be Muslims. The practice of any religion other than Islam is prohibited by law in the Country.

However, foreign residents are allowed to practice their religion if they do so privately. On July 4, the commemoration of the day the country embraced Islam, President Gayoom stated that no other religion should be allowed in the country, and the Home Affairs Ministry announced special programs to safeguard and strengthen religious unity. The President, the members of the People's Majlis, and cabinet members must be Muslims. There are no places of worship for adherents of other religions. The Government prohibits the importation of icons and religious statues, but it generally permits the importation of individual religious literature, such as Bibles, for personal use. It also prohibits non-Muslim clergy and missionaries from proselytising and conducting public worship services. Conversion of a Muslim to another faith is a violation of Shari'a and may result in a loss of the convert's citizenship.

Islamic instruction is a mandatory part of the school curriculum, and the Government funds the salaries of religious instructors. The Government has established a Supreme Council of Islamic Affairs to provide guidance on religious matters. The Government also has set standards for individuals who conduct Friday services at mosques to ensure adequate theological qualifications.

During June 1998, the authorities detained 24 foreigners

(including children) for alleged Christian proselytisation without explaining the charges against them and then expelled them from the country for life. Following the expulsion of the foreigners, police took two female citizens into custody for allegedly converting to Christianity. As many as a dozen other citizens were questioned. The women were detained from mid-June to late September 1998, during which time they received extensive counselling.

In April 1998, the Government asked the Seychelles Government to stop the radio broadcast of Christian programming in the local language, Dhivehi, to the country. However, the broadcasts continued throughout the year. Citizens are free to travel at home and abroad, to emigrate, and to return. Because of overcrowding, the Government discourages migration into the capital island of Male or its surrounding atoll. Foreign workers are often kept at their worksites. Their ability to travel freely is restricted, and they are not allowed to mingle with the local population on the islands. The Government has not formulated a policy regarding refugees, asylees, or first asylum. The issue of the provision of first asylum did not arise during the year.

There were no reports of forced expulsion of those having a valid claim to refugee status Citizens' ability to change their government is constrained, and the strong executive exerts significant influence over both the legislature and the judiciary. Under the 1997 Constitution, the Majlis chooses a single presidential nominee, who must be a Sunni Muslim male, from a list of self-announced candidates for the nomination. Would-be nominees for President are not permitted to campaign for the nomination. The nominee is then confirmed or rejected by secret ballot in a nationwide referendum. From a field of five candidates, President Gayoom was nominated by the Majlis and was confirmed for a fifth 5-year term in October 1998. Observers from the South Asian Association for Regional Cooperation(SAARC) found the referendum to be free and fair.

The elected members of the Majlis, who must be Muslims, serve 5-year terms. All citizens over 21 years of age may vote. Of the body's 50 members, 42 are elected--2 from each of the 20 inhabited atolls and 2 from Male--and the President appoints 8 members. Individuals or groups are free to approach members of the Majlis with grievances or opinions on proposed legislation, and any member may introduce legislation. There are no political parties, which are officially discouraged. The Office of the President is the most powerful political institution. The 1997 Constitution gives Islamic The Republic of Maldives, which comprises 1,190 islands (less than 200 of which are inhabited), with a population of approximately 270,000, has a parliamentary form of government with a very strong executive. The President appoints the Cabinet, members of the judiciary, and one-sixth of the Parliament. The President derives additional influence from his constitutional role as the "supreme authority to propagate the tenets" of Islam.

Political parties are officially discouraged, and candidates for the unicameral legislature, the People's Majlis, run as individuals. The Majlis selects a single presidential nominee who is approved or rejected in a national referendum. President Gayoom was approved for a fifth 5-year term in October 1998. The Majlis must approve all legislation and is empowered to enact legislation without presidential approval. Civil law is subordinate to Islamic law, but civil law generally is applied in criminal and civil cases. The judiciary is subject to executive influence.

The National Security Service (NSS) performs its duties under effective civilian control. The NSS includes the armed forces and police, and its members serve in both police and military capacities during their careers. The police division investigates crimes, collects intelligence, makes arrests, and enforces house arrest. Fishing, small-scale agriculture, and tourism provide employment for over one-half of the work force.

Tourism accounts for over one-quarter of government revenues and roughly 40 per cent of foreign exchange receipts. Manufacturing accounts for 6 per cent of gross domestic product.law pre-eminence over civil law and designates the President as the "supreme authority to propagate the tenets" of Islam.

The President's authority to appoint one-sixth of the Majlis members, which is one-third of the total needed for nominating the President, provides the President with a power base and strong political leverage. The President currently also is commander in chief of the armed forces, the Minister of Defence and National Security, the Minister of Finance and Treasury, and the Governor of the Maldivian Monetary Authority.

Role of Women

Women are not eligible to become president but may hold other government posts. For reasons of tradition and culture, few women seek or are selected for public office, and women are under represented in government and politics. In order to increase participation by women in the political process, the Government continued a political awareness campaign in the atolls. In the November 1999 elections, six women ran for seats and two were elected.

During the 1999 elections, observers from the SAARC noted that women participated equally in the electoral process. Following the elections, President Gayoom appointed an additional three women to the Majlis. Section 4 Governmental Attitude Regarding International and Non-governmental Investigation of Alleged Violations of Human Rights. Although not prohibited, there are no active local human rights groups. The Government has been responsive to at least one foreign government's interest in examining human rights issues. The Government also facilitated visits of teams of SAARC election observers in 1994, 1998, and 1999.

The 1997 Constitution declares all citizens equal before the law, but there is no specific provision to prohibit discrimination based on these factors. Women have traditionally been disadvantaged, particularly in terms of education and the application of Islamic law to matters such as divorce, inheritance, and testimony in legal proceedings.

Women's rights advocates agree that wife beating and other forms of violence are not widespread. There are no firm data on the extent of violence against women because of the value attached to privacy in this conservative society. In 1997 the Government commissioned a study by a local non-governmental organisation (NGO) on domestic violence, but it was never completed. Police officials report that they receive few complaints of assaults against women. Rape and other violent crimes against women are extremely rare. None were reported or prosecuted during the year. Under Shari'a the penalty would be flogging, banishment, or imprisonment for up to 5 years.

Women traditionally have played a subordinate role in society, although they now participate in public life in growing numbers and gradually are participating at higher levels. Women constitute 38 per cent of government employees, and about 10 per cent of uniformed NSS personnel. Well-educated women maintain that cultural norms, not the law, inhibit women's education and career choices. In many instances, education for girls is curtailed after the seventh grade, largely because parents do not allow girls to leave their home island for an island having a secondary school. Nonetheless, women enjoy a higher literacy rate (98 per cent) than men (96 per cent).

Due largely to orthodox Islamic training, there is a strong strain of conservative sentiment--especially among small businessmen and residents of the outer islands--that opposes an active role for women outside the home. However, the Government continued legal literacy programs to make women aware of their legal rights and workshops on gender and political awareness in the outer atolls.

The Government also has built 10 of 15 planned women's centres in the atolls, which are facilities where family health workers can provide medical services. The centres also provide libraries and space for meetings and other activities with a focus of the development of women. Under Islamic practice, husbands may divorce their wives more easily than vice versa, absent any mutual agreement to divorce. Islamic law also governs intestate inheritance, granting male heirs twice the share of female heirs.

Women who work for wages receive pay equal to that of men in the same positions. In October the Cabinet replaced the National Women's Council with a Gender Equality Council to serve as an advisory body to the Government to help strengthen the role of women in society and to help ensure equal participation by women in the country's development. Also during the year, the Government, with the assistance of the European Union and the UN Population Fund, expanded a program of small loans to women for development projects to additional islands.

The Government does not have a program of compulsory education, but it provides universal access to free primary education. The percentage of school-age children actually in school was as follows: (grades 1 to 5) 99.26 per cent, (grades 6 to 7) 96.2 per cent, and grades (8 to 10) 51.09 per cent. Of the students enrolled, 49 per cent are female and 51 per cent are male. The Government is committed to the protection of children's rights and welfare. The Government is working with UNICEF to implement the rights provided for in the UN Convention on the Rights of the Child. The Government established a National Council for the Protection of the Rights of the Child in 1992.

Government policy provides for equal access to educational and health programs for both male and female children. Laws protecting children's rights apply with equal force to children of either sex. Children's rights are incorporated into law, which specifically protects them from both physical and psychological abuse, including abuse at the hands of teachers or parents.

Ministry of Women's Affairs Social Welfare

The Ministry of Women's Affairs and Social Welfare has the authority to enforce this law, takes its responsibility seriously, and has received strong popular support for its efforts. The Ministry noted an increase in reports of child abuse during the first part of the year with 138 reports involving 317 children, including 10 reports of sexual abuse. Penalties could be banishment or imprisonment for up to 3 years. It is not known if there were any prosecutions during the year. The Government is reviewing the law to see if improvements and additional protections are necessary. There is no reported societal pattern of abuse directed against children.

There is no law that specifically addresses the rights of the physically or mentally disabled. In 1999 the Government initiated a survey and identified 30,000 persons in the country as disabled (primarily hearing and sight impaired). The Government has established programs and provided services for the disabled. Persons with disabilities usually are cared for by their families. When such care is unavailable, persons with disabilities are kept in the Institute for Needy People, which also assists elderly persons. The Government provides free medication for all mentally ill persons in the islands, and mobile teams regularly visit mentally ill patients.

In 1999 the Government enacted a new building code, which mandated that all new government buildings and jetties must be accessible to disabled persons. The CARE Society, an NGO that assists the disabled, with funding from UNICEF and the Australian Government, began programs to train disabled persons in life and work skills. While the Government does not expressly prohibit unions, it recognises neither the right to form them nor the right to strike. There were no reports of efforts to form unions or of strikes during the year. However, small groups of similarly employed workers with mutual interests have formed associations, which include employers as well as employees. These associations may address a variety of issues, including workers' rights. The work force consists of between 70,000 and 75,000 persons, including expatriate labour and seasonal and part-time workers. About 20 per cent of the workforce are employed in fishing.

Foreign Workers

The approximately 27,000 foreigners who work in the country make-up almost half of the workers in the formal sector; most are employed in tourist hotels, the retail and wholesale trade, factories, or on construction projects. The Government employs approximately 22,000 persons, both permanent and temporary. It estimates that the manufacturing sector employs about 15 per cent of the labour force and tourism another 10 per cent.

Although workers can affiliate with international labour federations, this generally has not been the case. However, it is believed some seamen have joined such federations.

In 1995 the US Government suspended Maldives' eligibility for tariff preferences under the US Generalised System of Preferences because the Government failed to take steps to afford internationally recognised worker rights to Maldivian workers. The law neither prohibits nor protects workers' rights to organise and bargain collectively. Wages in the private sector are set by contract between employers and employees and are usually based on the rates for similar work in the public sector.

There are no laws specifically prohibiting anti-union discrimination by employers against union members or organisers. The Government has exerted pressure in the past to discourage seamen from joining foreign seamen's unions as a means to secure higher wages. There have been no reported complaints alleging such discrimination or claiming government interference with workers' attempts to join unions in the past 5 years. Forced or compulsory labour is not prohibited by law. However, there were no reports that it occurred. The Government does not specifically prohibit forced and bonded labour by children, but such practices are not known to occur.

There is no compulsory education law, but more than 98 per cent of school-age children to grade 7 are enrolled in school. A 1992 law bars children under 14 years of age from "places of waged work and from work that is not suitable for that child's age, health, or physical ability or that might obstruct the education or adversely affect the mentality or behaviour of the child." An earlier law prohibits government employment of children under the age of 16.

There are no reports of children being employed in the small industrial sector, although children work in family fishing, agricultural, and commercial activities. The hours of work of young workers are not limited specifically by statute. The Government does not prohibit specifically forced and bonded labour by children, but such practices are not known to occur.

A Unit for Children's Rights in the Ministry of Women's Affairs and Social Welfare is responsible for monitoring compliance with the child labour regulations. It relies upon complaints filed with it rather than initiating its own inspections to ensure compliance. As a result, oversight is incomplete.

In 1994 the Government promulgated its first set of regulations for employer-employee relations. The regulations specify the terms that must be incorporated into employment contracts and address such issues as training, work hours, safety, remuneration, leave, fines, termination, etc. There is no national minimum wage for the private sector, although the

Government has established wage floors for certain kinds of work. Given the severe shortage of labour, employers must offer competitive pay and conditions to attract skilled workers.

There are no statutory provisions for hours of work, but the regulations require that a work contract specify the normal work and overtime hours on a weekly or monthly basis. In the public sector, a 7-hour day and a 5-day workweek have been established through administrative circulars from the President's office. Overtime pay in the public sector was instituted in 1990.

Employees are authorised 20 days of annual leave, 30 days of medical leave, maternity leave of 60 days, and special annual leave of 10 days for extraordinary circumstances. There are no laws governing health and safety conditions. However, there are regulatory requirements that employers provide a safe working environment and ensure the observance of safety measures. Most South Asians are now citizens of democratic states. There has been increased decentralisation in political power. These are important steps forward for a region characterised by diversity of religion ethnicity, class, caste and language. India, Pakistan and Bangladesh comprise over 95 per cent of South Asia's total population.

Both Bangladesh and India are now democratically ruled, and Pakistan, having recently reverted to military rule after 11 years of elected governments, hopes to be heading back towards democracy in the near future. India and Sri Lanka have never had any form of government that was not democratically elected.

Conversely, Pakistan had been ruled by the military for 26 of its 52 years as an independent country, while Bangladesh has been under military rule for 17 of its 28 years of independence. These countries have spent the majority of the last decade under some form of democratically elected government. The existence of elected governments alone is not the sole criterion for judging the extent of political progress.

Indeed, all South Asian countries have been witness to a growth of institutions of governance that promise to articulate the demands of people from the grassroots. These include, for example, the panchayats in India, and the elected provincial councils of Sri Lanka. These institutions are representative bodies at the local level that allow people to take an active role in addressing their own concerns.

The main threat to the efficient working of political institutions is the pervasive inequalities that persist in South Asian societies, manifested through powerful elite groups which often use these institutions to serve their personal interests. But the great importance of these fledgling local level institutions of governance should not be understated. Another vital element in the maturing of the political process in the region has been civil society organisations (CSOs). These are responsible for numerous, innovative initiatives to improve local level governance. Among the oft-quoted examples include Province and North and Central Punjab than in Southern Punjab and interior Sindh in Pakistan. This is because the social, cultural and economic barriers to such initiatives are much more powerful in the latter areas. These areas are commonly associated with the persistence of the traditional feudal system characterised by a few large land-holding estates and masses of, smallholding farmers and landless peasants.

In any case, the prospects for continuing progress are good, so long as the successful efforts are acknowledged and continue to be used as benchmarks for other initiatives. No single era of South Asian history has been witness to such rapid advances in health, education, nutrition and human development in general. When discussing human development in the region, Sri Lanka and the Maldives stand out due to their impressive initiatives in the social sectors.

With over 90 per cent of adults literate, these countries have achieved one of the primary prerequisites to long-term and pervasive economic and human development. The other countries in the region, while still far from having adequate education facilities and attainment levels, have managed to make substantial headway into the problem of reducing illiteracy. The South Asian region had witnessed a dramatic progress in the area of public health. Access to basic preventive health-care has also resulted in dramatically reducing mortality rates.

In 1980, the South Asian average for one-year olds that had been fully immunised against tuberculosis and measles was 13 per cent and one per cent respectively, and in 1997 these figures were 95 per cent and 79 per cent. Infant mortality rates have dropped by 65 per cent in Nepal and 51 per cent in India.

In 1998, all South Asian countries had succeeded in reducing infant mortality rates to below 100 per 1, 000 live births, compared to 1960 when only Sri Lanka at 90, had such a rate. The improvements are the result of policies directed towards achieving human development goals. Concern for human development has not been enough of a priority for most policy makers in the region. The result is that there are now increasing absolute numbers of people without adequate health and sanitation, more undernourished children, and more and more people who are functionally illiterate.

Prosperous Future

A prosperous future for South Asia is dependent on the solution of these problems, and a commitment to ensuring that all South Asians attain a decent and dignified standard of living. The annual growth rate of GNP in South Asia between 1975 and 1995 was three per cent which is second in the world only to East Asia. However, when one looks beyond these basic figures, it is clear that there has been little in the way of actual improvements in standards of living for the majority of people.

With the exception of India, which has been relatively successful in poverty reduction efforts, and continues to be so, the rest of South Asia has witnessed increasing poverty since the late 1980s. Indeed, the growth rate quoted above falls drastically to 2.2 per cent when India is excluded, and in fact, in real terms, excluding India again, South Asia's per capita annual growth rate in the same time-frame is actually minus 0.3 per cent. The numbers of absolute poor in the region have increased from 270 million people in the 1960s to approximately 515 million people in 1995. Ninety per cent of rural Bhutanese live below the poverty line.

Pakistan has witnessed an increase in the Gini coefficient of inequality from 0.35 in 1987 to 0.42 in 1994, with its lowest income group suffering a decline in real income to the tune of 56 per cent since the late 1980s. The reasons for this continuing anti-poor growth are many, but most can be attributed to wholly inappropriate policies and poor governance, which have resulted in corruption, fiscal irresponsibility, and increasing poverty and unemployment.

South Asia is home to most of the out-of-school, children in the world. Bhutan's net enrolment ratio at the primary level is a dismal 13.2 per cent, while Bangladesh has 21.6 per cent enrolled at the secondary level. Both of these figures are well below the least developed country averages of 60.4 per cent and 31.2 per cent respectively. Adult literacy has only increased from 17 per cent to 49 per cent between 1970 and 1995 compared to 71 per cent for developing countries as a whole. Dropout rates are also high.[8]

Many South Asians—often pressed by acute economic need—decide not to invest in education because there seems to be little reward to doing so. In particular, the current employment situation in countries like Pakistan and Sri Lanka is the worst for the educated youth. In this regard, vocational and technical training are essential to ensure that South Asian youths are trained in job-oriented skills to meet the challenges of the new world. In South Asia, child and maternal mortality rates are still high. Diseases such as malaria and tuberculosis are staging a comeback, and the new, frightening AIDS epidemic is becoming a major health problem.

Unfortunately, there is limited documentation of AIDS cases in South Asia, primarily because, there is little awareness among large parts of the population about the disease, its symptoms, and its treatment. There is also a serious social taboo associated with the disease, which ensures that it is rarely talked about in public. In India, which has the largest number of HIV positive cases in the region at a reported four million, there seem to be more concrete measures being taken to deal with the problem through the setting up of counselling centres, emergency facilities and the like.

There are still vast numbers of people without access to proper health, education, and sanitation facilities, in South Asia. Public expenditure on the social sectors continues to be insufficient. The lack of political will demonstrated by those making policies cannot be understated. Sri Lanka, long noted for its superior human development record, has also cut social sector expenditure in recent years: its public expenditure on health as a percentage of GDP has decreased from two per cent to 1.4 per cent between 1960 and 1995.

The basic human needs are not being met is indicative of how the problem of underdevelopment still persists, and that too, in massive proportions. Alongside human deprivation, there is the frightening prospect of deterioration of the environment, which, if allowed to continue, threatens to permanently damage ecological systems. Pakistan has the eighth worst annual rate of deforestation in the world at 2.9 per cent. Since the 1980s, there have been limited improvements in environmental practices in South Asia with the exception of initiatives of the non-government sector such as the Chipko movement in India. Unsustainable practices can be attributed to two basic factors. First, there is the scant disregard that some interest groups pay to the environment.

For example, land mafias, timber mafias and large-scale industrialists are often unconcerned about how their profiteering will affect the present and future generations who rely on natural resources for their livelihoods. They also ignore the very basic problem of depletion of the natural resource base. The other reason for ecological degradation is poverty.

The vast numbers of poor people in the region are starved for sustainable livelihoods and a combination of this basic need and a lack of awareness leads to their engagement in practices that harm the environment. This vicious cycle of poverty and environmental degradation is lethal: it is indeed one of South Asia's major concerns that long-term pressures on grasslands due to rapid growth in human and livestock populations is resulting in biodiversity loss. Urban migration is becoming a major problem in South Asian cities. Labour surplus in rural areas in South Asia had led to a constant flow of migrants to urban areas. This has resulted in the explosion of mega-cities in the region. The result has been the mushrooming of slums and squatter settlements. Among other social and economic ills these slum areas are often breeding grounds for diseases due to poor-health and sanitation facilities.

In large cities such as Calcutta, Dhaka, Kolkota, and Karachi, millions of people reside in illegal squatter settlements, predominantly on government-owned land. These slum areas are provided with basic amenities arbitrarily and often through an intricate web of corrupt government official and land mafias. These settlements then expand rapidly as these are the only real viable housing options for new low-income migrants.

At the same time, later generations of slum dwellers also need to find space for increasingly large families. The state's failure to meet the needs of poor people is conveniently hidden from time to time by large-scale demolitions of these slums. This has happened across the region. The reason behind such demolitions is unclear, while on the one hand, these operations may temporarily clear the city of settlements, they do not address the long-term issue of inadequate housing facilities for the poor. Government policies with regard to such settlements are often inconsistent—they are left alone, even encouraged to flourish for decades, and then they are arbitrarily torn down when it is thought appropriate with no thought for the human cost.

Another interesting phenomenon is the large vote bank that these slums represent. As these are concentrated settlements comprising large proportions of city populations, they can be great sources of political power. This means that politicians will cater to the needs of the slum dwellers only when it is in their interest to do so. The responses from slum dwellers to reactionary policies on the part of the government have varied. There have been large-scale rallies and demonstrations in Dhaka against forced evictions, resulting in a High Court decision decreeing that evictions defied basic principles of human rights and dignity. Efforts to truly address this problem have rested primarily with civil society groups.

The well documented successes of the Orangi Pilot Project (OPP) in Pakistan and SSM in Sri Lanka stand out. However, there have been some government initiatives such as the Sindh Katchi Abadi Authority (SKAA) which has been quite successful in organising slum residents and working towards long-term housing settlement.

South Asia is one of the most poorly governed regions in the world. For example, the formal institutions of governance in the region often bypass the many unfortunate people who suffer from multiple deprivations on account of their income, religion, gender and ethnicity. The poor have not only been excluded from the benefits of growth but have also failed to gain political empowerment. Some of the worst consequences of their exclusion are seen in the high rates of crime and violence throughout the region. Income disparities in South Asia are amongst the largest in the world. The richest one-fifth of South Asians earn almost 40 per cent of the region's income, while the poorest one-fifth earns less than 10 per cent.

Elections are often the only bridge between the state and society. People continually feel excluded from the larger political process through which decisions that directly affect their livelihoods are made. The dominance of a narrow band of elite reflects the concentrated nature of political power. The concentration and personalisation of state power has coincided with the parallel erosion of institutions of governance. Institutional decay is evident in parliaments that cannot protect peoples interests, in civil services that are heavily politicised and unable to provide basic public services. South Asian countries are suffering from inefficient systems of economic management. Most taxes are regressive, falling far more on the poor and the middle class than on the rich, because nearly 70 per cent of the region's total tax revenue is obtained through levying indirect taxes. This crushing burden of taxation on the poor is not only enormous, but also increasing. In many countries direct taxes as a proportion of GDP have actually fallen in the last decade, while huge sectors of society remain under-taxed or untaxed.

The bulk of public spending in South Asia goes to providing non-merit subsidies, making up the losses of public corporations, and maintaining a large force of civil servants and the military. Total public debt as a percentage of GDP is over 60 per cent in Pakistan, Nepal, Sri Lanka and India, although most of India's debt is domestic rather than external. Evidence of corruption in South Asia is widespread: in reduced availability and increased cost of basic social services, in allocation of resources for mega-projects, and in the breakdown of the rule of law.

South Asian region has had a precarious employment situation. The most recent official unemployment rate for Sri Lanka stands at 11.3 per cent. Real wages in the manufacturing and agricultural sectors have declined considerably in the period between 1980 and 1995. In Pakistan in the 1990s, with lower output growth and fewer people migrating abroad, the employment situation has worsened significantly. In Bangladesh, which has experienced high levels of urban labour absorption and fairly high levels of growth in the same period, there are still insufficient jobs to counter the numbers of people joining the labour force.

Women in South Asia are the worst off, contending with exclusionary practices embedded in society from the time they are born. The human costs of poor governance, regional economic non-cooperation and military confrontation are heavier on women of the region. Women bear the brunt of the lives lost as a result or disease, hunger, civil and military strife and poverty.

Women and girls in the region face discrimination in access to health, education, employment, and in all other areas. In addition, they are the victims of some oppressive land, rigid customs and traditions that perpetuate their disadvantage. They bear children, early and often, and are pressured to produce sons rather than daughters. Many perish in the process.

A weak judicial system fails to uphold women's right, and, struggling economics provide opportunities predominantly for men. The lack of regional cooperation and the relentless forces of globalisation combine to put a further squeeze on poor women working in the informal sector, as large corporations swallow up small entrepreneurs.

Role of SAARC

South Asia has yet to come together as a region in order to reap the benefits that come with regional economic integration. The South Asian Association for Regional Cooperation (SAARC) was South Asia's attempt to create unity within the region. Set up in 1985, SAARC had not made any significant headway by way of regional economic integration.

So far SAARC has only one real achievement—the setting up of the South Asian Preferential Trade Agreement (SAPTA) in 1993. SAPTA was envisioned to lead to the formation of a South Asian Free Trade Area (SAFTA). The agreement, which took effect in December 1995, was very cautious and was based on product-by-product tariff reductions.

The actual extent of trade and cooperation within the South Asia region has declined steadily, except for some minimal increase between India and Nepal. The averages, however, are highly skewed by the trade patterns of India and Pakistan since they are the two largest economies in the region. The lack of cooperation within SAARC prevails in an environment where it is clear that there is much to be gained from cooperation in terms of poverty reduction, social sector development, tourism, energy, transport and communication.

At the tenth SAARC Summit in Colombo in 1995, a Social Charter was proposed to deal with many social issues and with combining efforts to address the many deprivations faced by the largely poor, uneducated, and under-served populations in the region. Despite this, actual progress has been limited. There have been many analysis showing the efficiency gains from cooperation. Empirical studies on the trade of India, Pakistan, Bangladesh and Sri Lanka find that expanded cooperation benefits all countries, in particular with regard to GNP growth. Two separate studies to determine the effects of a possible regional trade agreement in South Asia have shown trade and welfare enhancing effect. The main findings indicate that high transport costs associated with internal trade in the larger countries and with partners outside the region, can be lowered by increasing intra-regional trade. Furthermore, new trade in goods and services can be generated that could have a significant growth-enhancing effect.

There is reason to believe that there are some sectors that would gain considerably by regional integration. Cooperation in sectors such as gas and electricity could be substantial. In addition, there is potential for trade in manufacturing inputs that would reduce energy price stocks.

Estimates of demand and substitution elasticities for manufacturing sectors in Pakistan, India and Bangladesh indicate a high degree of substitutability among capital, labour and energy resources. Higher energy prices can be partially compensated for by greater use of non-energy inputs, specifically both capital and labour in India and Pakistan. Labour abundance in both countries is a factor that encourages this adjustment. The trade to capital inputs is likely to benefit both countries also. South Asian nations have much to gain from increasing trade cooperation, and opening borders to one another. The evidence does not even take up into account the non-trade barriers that are likely to be removed in the context of regional agreement. The constraints of regional cooperation are all too evident. Neither India nor Pakistan have been able to establish stable relationship with one another. Constant tension has put pressures on the region which have undermined peace, prosperity and progress. Sri Lanka too has been embroiled in a civil war which has crippled the country and has almost entirely overshadowed its otherwise tremendous human development record.

While there are other potential bottlenecks to regional cooperation, such as underdeveloped communication links and infrastructures, these are rapidly improving, and are not nearly as large an impediment to cooperation as is the perennial conflict between the countries of the region. The spiralling of conflict into nuclearisation of the region has intensified the problem.

The nuclear tests conducted by India and Pakistan in April and May 1998 have further compromised human welfare in the region. The only hope of improving the strained relations between South Asian countries—and this extends to beyond just the Indo-Pak situation—is to highlight the immense gains that are possible if South Asia focuses on mutual cooperation.

Population movements can also be perceived by governments to enhance their security and well-being. Sending states may use migration for the purposes of asserting either formal sovereignty or *de facto* control over a territory. This policy involves governmental encouragement of civilian rather than military movement into claimed territories for the purposes of establishing effective control. Sending states can also actively use population movements or 'push-outs' as tools in their foreign policies.

The export of refugees can also be used as a bargaining chip in interstate negotiations over trade and bilateral political recognition. Typically in such situations the sending state possesses considerable leverage in the bargaining process. By pleading an inability to control the population outflow, or by demonstrating a willingness to manipulate it, the sending state is in a position to extract foreign policy and strategic concessions from the receiving state. Population movements are seen as contributing to the host state's power base, national self-confidence or dominant ethnic community.

Population influxes can also augment or increase the size of the receiving state's defence capabilities or military establishment. Security can no longer be viewed as an independent national problem based on limited self-interest, and that problems of forced migration can no longer be viewed from the limited humanitarian perspective has significantly broadened the agenda of international relations. The UN Security Council's Summit Declaration of 31 January 1992 acknowledged that threats to international peace and security can originate from non-military sources of instability in the economic, social, humanitarian and ecological fields, and that such conflicts fall within the Security Council's sphere of action.

The declaration also welcomed election-monitoring, human rights verification, and the repatriation of refugees as integral parts of the Security Council's efforts to maintain international peace and security. These expanded notions of what constitute threats to international security have resulted in new international actions to deal with human rights violations which generate forced migration on a large scale.

The South Asian region is emerging as the poorest, the most illiterate, the most malnourished and the least gender-sensitive region in the world. The causes of the exoduses of 1947-48 and 1971, can clearly be identified as violent communal conflict associated in both cases with the process of state formation. The other involuntary movements mentioned above can broadly be ascribed to human rights violations, resulting from the existence of elite-dominated political systems and a pervasive climate of religious and ethnic intolerance reinforced by high levels of poverty, landlessness and unemployment.

Unless there are determined efforts to address the causes of mass displacement, South Asia could well be the scene of further refugee exoduses in the years to come. Meaningful political reforms are needed to ensure that violence both by the state and by non-state actors is uncompromisingly subordinated to the rule of law. As well as increasing in scale, the geographical scope of forced displacement can also be said to have widened in recent years. But this trend is not a simple one.

During the past decade, a number of conflicts and associated problems of forced displacement have been resolved. At the same time, however, new crises have exploded in regions which were previously unaffected by the problem of forced displacement or where involuntary population movements did not come to the attention of the international community.

South Asia, which is rarely recognised as a 'refugee-affected' region, has in recent years witnessed a succession of cross-border movements: from Bhutan and Tibet to Nepal; from Myanmar to Bangladesh and Thailand; and from Bhutan, Sri Lanka and Tibet to India. According to one recent estimate, moreover, the 750,000 people in South Asia who are currently protected and assisted by UNHCR constitute less than half of all the displaced people in the subcontinent.

In a number of locations around the world, whole 'neighbourhoods' of states have become affected by interlocking and mutually reinforcing patterns of armed conflict and forced displacement. This phenomenon can be observed in the Caucasus, for example, a region which includes no fewer than six entities which have produced refugees and displaced people: Abkhazia, Armenia, Azerbaijan, Chechnya, North and South Ossetia. It can also be seen in Central Africa, where forced population displacements have recently taken place within and between nine contiguous states: Angola, Burundi, Central African Republic, Congo, Rwanda, Tanzania, Uganda, Zaire and Zambia.

As these examples suggest, forced population displacements are becoming increasingly complex. Movements of refugees and internally displaced people now often criss-cross each other, collecting and discarding people on the way. At the same time, there would appear to be a growing number of situations in which people are repeatedly uprooted, expelled or relocated within and across state borders, forcing them to live a desperately insecure and nomadic existence.

During the past few years, a growing proportion of the

people who have succeeded in escaping from their own country have found that their new situation is just as—if not more— insecure than the one they left behind. Paradoxically, in an era when so many people have become the victims of ethnic cleansing and other forms of mass expulsion, many others have found it impossible to escape from their own country and to find refuge elsewhere.

In some case cases, as in Sri Lanka, for example, their departure has been blocked by government or opposition forces who wish to maintain control over the civilian population. Diaspora communities, many of which are themselves the product of forced population displacements, have played an important part in maintaining the volume and determining the direction of such migratory movements. The Tamil who decides to leave Sri Lanka, will almost invariably make use of information, resources and contacts provided by compatriots in Europe or North America in the bid to leave his or her homeland.

A number of trends appear to have contributed to the growing scale and speed of forced displacement in various parts of the world: the emergence of new forms of warfare, entailing the destruction of whole social, economic and political systems; the spread of light weapons and landmines, available at prices which enable whole populations—including their youngest members—to be armed; and, perhaps most significantly, the use of mass evictions and expulsions as a weapon of war and as a means of establishing culturally or ethnically homogeneous societies. The large scale of some population displacements and migratory movements can be attributed to a form of mass desperation, provoked by very rapid processes of social, political and economic change. Commenting upon such developments, the UN High Commissioner for Refugees has observed that "the forced displacement of minorities, including depopulation and repopulation tactics in support of territorial claims and self-determination, has become an abominable characteristic of the contemporary world."

In some countries, the tactic of rural depopulation has been used to permit the theft of cattle, property and other assets, whereas in other situations, such as Afghanistan, Sri

Lanka, civilian populations have been forcibly dispersed or relocated for primarily political reasons, so as to deprive rebel movements of their natural supporters. The present conflict may result in the flight of Mujahirs to India. This is evident from the mood of the people coming from Pakistan these days, who now blame the partition for their plight and express preference for returning to India as they do not expect to get justice and fair treatment in Pakistan. There is the developing situation in Myanmar, after the release of the leader of the Democracy Movement Aung San Suu Kyi in July 1995. The thrust of her statements has been that the political crisis of democracy in Myanmar be resolved through talks and national reconciliation. This could also be the wish of Myanmar's present and future foreign investors.

However, the sticking point between the Democracy Movement and the military regime—the State Law and Order Reorganisation Committee (SLORC)—is that military must have an important constitutional position in Myanmar's political system. This is not acceptable to the leaders of the Democracy Movement. If an amicable way out is not found to this problem, the revival of conflict between the SLORC and the Democracy Movement, and the reintensification of insurgency and ethnic conflict may generate refugee flows from Myanmar to its neighbours including those in South Asia. The emerging ethnic and regional tensions in Nepal would be absorbed and accommodated with the demographic framework of polity but if not, then any outbreak of conflict on these divisive lines would produce refugees. India would be the only destination of these refugees, particularly from the Limbuwan region because of socio-cultural identities of Rais, Limbus, Magars and Gurungs across the border in India where there is concentration of Indian Nepalis in North Bengal and Sikkim. Democratic politics in Nepal promises to play a positive role in diffusing ethnic tensions by channelising them through political parties, media, non-governmental organisations and even parliament.

There is, no scope for complacency as some regions of Nepal are not free from regional and ethnic problems, and similar developments in India tend to activist-sectarian identities which cut across national boundaries of the two neighbours. In addition to these potential conflicts becoming a source of refugees in South Asia, there are also prospects of economic migration increasing in the region in the years to come.

The UNHCR reported a return of 103,000 refugees from Pakistan to Afghanistan during 1994, even in the midst of reintensified conflict. This could be possible, perhaps because the fighting was confined mostly to Kabul and its vicinity, and the refugees belonging to other areas could go back. Similarly, the Bangladesh government, with the help of the UNHCR could help 82,860 Rohingyas return to their villages in Myanmar during the later half of 1994. There has been a significant shift in South Asia since the mid-sixties, in the context of repatriation. Earlier there was a greater willingness to accept refugees and rehabilitate them without making efforts for their repatriation. This was clearly the case with regard to the refugees that crossed Indian and Pakistani borders in 1947 and later on.

India also accepted refugees coming from Sri Lanka and Myanmar during the early sixties.

During partition, it was accepted by both the countries that that the displaced people were the responsibility of the host country, notwithstanding the fact that India had not endorsed the two-nation theory that sought to divide states on the basis of religion. India, also, it seems had either accepted its moral responsibility or found it politically prudent in the aftermath of conflict with China to rehabilitate the refugees from Myanmar and Sri Lanka.

India and other South Asian countries had also accepted refugees coming from Tibet since the early fifties, possibly, as a result of political decision to make use of them strategically in their relations with communist China.

Gradually, the South Asian countries have become more and more unwilling to accept refugees coming from their neighbours. Even when Pakistan has made a strategic use of the Afghan refugees and India of the East Pakistan and Sri Lankan refugees, the efforts have been to send them back soon after the strategic value of the refugees was lost and the burden of their presence became an economic, administrative and political liability. Now the shift in the global attitude towards the refugees, ot "keeping would-be refugees at home" has also strengthened the South Asian attitudes, not only to resist the incoming refugees but also to send those living for long time, back as soon as possible. It may be mentioned in this regard that almost every South Asian country—India, Pakistan, Bangladesh and Nepal—have even used force, either to stop refugees from coming, or to send them back, or in both the circumstances. Under a bilateral agreement with India, the Bangladesh government promised "a 16-point repatriation and reinteg-ration package that included financial assistance worth some $250" per individual, but on actual verification of conditions on ground, it was found that "less than half of the financial aid promised" had been given and other conditions had not been created for the repatriates to "settle in their places of origin."

The South Asian countries have pursued various strategies and actions to deal with the refugee problems and their respective security implications. At the local level two broad patterns of settlement adopted for the refugees are evident in South Asia. The host state has either kept the refugees in well defined camps at one place or kept the movements of the refugees somewhat restricted. Such settlement pattern, if maintained and regulated properly, may give rise to least difficulties, keeping the security implications manageable. Alternately, refugees have been dispersed to different areas, farther from their points of entry, and even among the local populations that do not share much of the socio-cultural identities with the asylum seekers. In such cases, refugees have also enjoyed a greater freedom of movement and activity, including seeking jobs and organising themselves politically.

The settlements of Afghan refugees in Pakistan and the Tamils of Sri Lanka in India may be mentioned here. Security risks and instances of instability caused by tensions between the local population and the refugees have been the largest and the most severe in such cases. In relation to the external dimension of the refugee question, the general and most natural strategy adopted by the host state has been to engage the home state in direct negotiations to resolve, and/or moderate the implications of the refugee presence.

The experience in South Asia shows that this strategy has been considerably successful in terms of its costs and results. Bilateral and negotiated agreements between India and Sri Lanka on the Tamil issue, the Myanmar and the Bangladeshi governments on the Rohingyas, and between India and Bangladesh on the Chakmas, may be mentioned in this regard. Such agreements have not been perfect and their implementation has often been tardy and cumbersome, resulting in slow and delayed resolution of the problem at hand. The Indian military intervention in arming the Mukti Bahini, and fighting a full-scale war with Pakistan which enabled the ten million and odd refugees to return to Bangladesh was initiated after the failure of other options. The then Prime Minister of India, Indira Gandhi, had clearly warned that "Pakistan cannot be allowed to seek a solution of its political or other problems at the expense of India and on the Indian soil".

The strategy of intervention and war was also evident in dealing with the crisis of Afghan refugees in Pakistan. The US, Western powers, their allies and China had all joined hands with Pakistan to force the Soviet military out of Afghanistan and thus create conditions for the return of refugees.

The qualitative difference in this situation with that of the Bangladesh conflict of 1971 was that while the intervention and war in Afghanistan was a part of the global Cold War and Sino-Soviet rivalry, in the 1971 conflict the host state alone was motivated into action to defend its interests.

The burden of the global rivalries in fact lent support to the home state, Pakistan, in 1971. The third instance of this drastic strategy in dealing with the refugee-generating conflict in South Asia was India's intervention and pressure on Sri Lanka. The Agreement of July 1987 aimed not only at securing conditions for the repatriation of refugees but also at resolving the ethnic conflict through a fair accommodation of Tamils' fights and interests. In all the instances of the use of war and intervention as a strategy to deal with the refugee issue, we must reiterate that return of the refugees was only one of the many objectives and motivating factors. This involved political use of refugees by the host state in pursuance of broader and diverse interests. It may also be kept in mind that this strategy only partially resolved the refugee-related concerns.

In the case of the emergence of Bangladesh, an unassessed number of refugees did get lost and were eventually absorbed in the vast Indian heartland, mixing with its teeming millions. The hopes of a very amicable relationship between India and Bangladesh also vanished after initial years when India started facing the pressure of economic and illegal migrants from Bangladesh.

In Afghanistan, the arms and militia forces raised during the war of attrition precipitated yet another internecine conflict which has not allowed all the refugees to repatriate. And in Sri Lanka, the 1987 Agreement and the political and military arrangements envisaged under this, ran into rough weather due to changing political dynamics in the two countries. The conflict in Sri Lanka has also been reintensified, leaving the unrepatriated refugees in the lurch.

Besides the partial and constrained efficacy of the strategy of war and intervention, this option is also not available to all. The weak and small countries are incapable of pursuing such a strategy either in relation to each other or *vis-a-vis* a strong and powerful neighbour. Thus a country like Nepal cannot take resort to this strategy either against Bhutan where negotiated solution does not hold much promise, at least for the time being, or against Tibet. Nepal is also not in a position to exercise pressure against India to stop the inflow of economic migrants. Nepal's repeated attempts to get the Indo-Nepal border movements regulated has not evoked any desirable responses from India.

The only South Asian regional organisation, SAARC, does not permit 'bilateral and contentious issues' to be brought on its agenda and as most of the refugee issues are bilateral and contentious in nature, SAARC cannot address them. There is a pressure for liberating SAARC from this disability of not discussing bilateral and contentious issues, particularly from countries like Pakistan, Bangladesh and Nepal. But this is a politically motivated pressure, not sincerely concerned with the resolution of problems and evolution of mutually accommodative solutions.

Notwithstanding this debate on the acceptance of 'bilateral and contentious issues', the fact remains that the SAARC forum and frequency of meetings at various senior bureaucratic and political levels have exercised a benign influence on the resolution of bilateral conflictual issues, including those related with the refugees. The Indo-Sri Lanka dialogue on the Tamil ethnic conflict during the 1986 SAARC Summit may be recalled. Similarly, talks between Nepali Prime Minister Koirala and the Bhutanese King on the question of the Bhutanese refugees in Nepal, during the Dhaka SAARC Summit in 1994, paved the way for bilateral negotiations between the two countries.

Almost all the South Asian states are afflicted by the refugee problem and in some cases, the refugee issues affect more than two countries. The Bhutanese refugees, for instance, are an issue both in India and Nepal. The Bangladeshi economic and illegal immigrants are present in India, Nepal and also Pakistan. There are also Bihari Muslims in Bangladesh who have proclaimed their loyalties to Pakistan but have not been able to go to their cherished land.

In addition, the security implications of refugee movements involve drug trafficking and terrorism, the areas which are already covered under a regional SAARC convention. Above all, if the refugee question is denuded from the political and strategic use of the refugees by either the home or the host state then much of its contentious and conflictual aspects will get moderated. On the lines of the SAARC Convention on Suppression of Drug Trafficking and Terrorism, a regional understanding on refugee-related issues may be evolved. Under the umbrella of such an understanding, security and other implications of the refugee movements may be more effectively addressed even in the bilateral context.

The real answer to the refugee problem lies in working at the national level to resolve such conflicts or diffuse such situations that produce refugees. For example, a resolution of ethnic conflict in Sri Lanka and Bhutan, or the ending of the power struggle in Afghanistan with the establishment of a stable political order, will make it far more easier to repatriate the refugees produced by all these conflicts. It is interesting to recall that the Indo-Sri Lanka Agreement of 1987 devoted considerable attention to the action on the part of the Sri Lankan government at the national level for resolving the ethnic conflict that had produced refugees.[11]

The Indo-Bangladesh understanding on the Chakma refugees repatriation also expected national action on the part of Bangladesh government whereby Muslims settled in CHT in the Chakma areas were to be shifted away.

Failure of the envisaged national actions both in Sri Lanka and Bangladesh vitiated the expectations on repatriation. But then, there may be no guarantee that such conflicts will not be created anew by the state and nation-building processes in South Asian countries. Throughout the centuries, people have been obliged to flee from their own country or community as a result of persecution, armed conflict and violence. And in part of the world, governments, armies and rebel movements have resorted to moving people by force in order to attain their political and military objectives.

The people most seriously affected by the problem of forced displacement are often the most marginalised members of society: minority groups, stateless people, indigenous populations and others who are excluded from the structures of political power. Persecuted by their governments or by other members of their society, many find themselves living in a state of constant insecurity and uncertainty.

In South Asia, the migration trends has two main periods of direct outflow and a third period of secondary movement. The first period is dominated by the Indenture movement. Indenture took place within the British imperial system but indenturing workers from British India was adopted in Dutch and French colonial territories as well. This period stretched from 1834 to 1920. The second main phase is that of the post-war period of free market migration.

This movement affected Britain in particular, but also the United States, Canada, some European countries and the Middle East. The third movement overlaps the last and shares with it many of the destinations. This is the secondary migration, often forced, of the descendants of the first phase of migration. The most spectacular of these movements was the expulsion of Asians from East Africa, but there were also expulsions or repatriations from Burma (now Myanmar) and Ceylon (now Sri Lanka) and political flights of South Asians from Surinam and Fiji. The timing of its inception, just after the

1833 emancipation of slaves in the British Empire, is not accidental: indenture replaced direct slavery. In the West Indies, sugar plantations were still being established in Trinidad and in British Guiana in the 1830s. The Dutch, at a later date, were engaged in similar developments in their part of Guyana and the French in the islands of Martinique and Guadeloupe.

Indenture was started in the French and Dutch colonies shortly after they abolished slavery. The French banned slavery in their colonies in 1848 and recruitment from their Indian colonies started in 1854 and from British India in 1861. The Dutch banned slavery even later, 1863, and started recruiting 'Hindustanis' in 1873. The banning of slavery by the British government, coupled with the rejection by Afro-Caribbeans of plantation work, made the West Indian planters search for new labour sources. Similar searches took place in Natal, Mauritius, Fiji and elsewhere. Land-hungry India provided the source. Indentured migration must therefore be seen as part of the imperialist and capitalist core-periphery relationship. In East Africa and Malaya, they went as railway builders and as administrators. In South Africa, they worked in the coal mines as well as on sugar and cotton plantations. Nor was indenture the only scheme of recruitment. Under the *Kangani* and *Maistri* systems, an Indian returning home was commissioned as a middleman to recruit labourers from his home district.

The *Kangani* system of labour recruitment was particularly important and replaced indenture in Malaya after that system was abolished there in 1910. There was also considerable movement of free migrants, traders, doctors and lawyers to areas where South Asian communities were settled. Seamen had been important migrants since the days of the East India Company and Lascar sailors had formed the nucleus of Bengali settlement in the East End of London. Finally, one should not overlook the importance of student movement and the settlement of scientists, doctors and academics in Britain.

Indenture generally required the emigrant to apprentice himself or herself to a master for five years, although a range from three to ten years is found. There were often additional conditions. In the case of Trinidad, the worker was indentured for five years but was obliged to work for a further five before he/she was eligible for a free return passage. At the end of this period he could either retire, passage paid, to his homeland or else take a piece of land to cultivate as his own in the overseas territory. These contractual promises were not always fulfilled. The Protectors, who were appointed by the Indian government, seem to have been fairly powerless. For whatever reasons, the return flow of formerly indentured workers was generally small. For example, of the 143, 939 Indians who migrated to Trinidad under indenture, only 33,294 eventually returned to India.

A considerable number of repatriated indentured migrants signed on for further periods in Trinidad. However, in Martinique and Guadeloupe, just under a third of the immigrants seem to have been repatriated and a similar rate is true of Surinam. The agreements between governments which controlled these contracts required women to be included in the indentured group in the ratio of 4 : 10. Women also seem to have had a shorter period of indenture—three rather than five years. The communities which resulted from indenture thus tended initially to have a skewed sex-ratio. 'Passenger Indians', on the other hand, tended to have a much more balanced structure so that in South Africa, for example, although passenger Indians constituted only 10 per cent of the migrants, their descendants now form 30 per cent of the current South Asian population in that country.

In Mauritius, Fiji and Guyana they came to constitute a majority, but only in Mauritius has that demographic fact been turned into democratic political control. In Fiji, the Constitution created by the British on independence guaranteed native Fijian control.

During British rule, South Asians also formed a middle class in Myanmar but independence brought ethnically exclusionary policies and forced many of them (the skilled service occupation sector in particular) out of the country. Only the poor South Asians continued to live there, keeping a low profile, adopting Myanmar dress and language in public.

Even here, however, Muslims along the border with India and Bangladesh were being forced out of the country in 1992. There is no clear findings to what extent the origins of the overseas South Asians reflect the balance of the population of the subcontinent. In the subcontinent, about three-quarters come from the Aryan north and about a quarter from the Dravidian south. Northerners (Punjabis and Gujaratis) are dominant in Britain, Canada and the British Caribbean. Tamils are prominent in the settlement of Malaysia, Singapore, and also in the French territories. Gujaratis and Punjabis were prominent in the East and South African settlements. Northerners, from Uttar Pradesh in particular, predominate among the Trinidad East Indians.

The movement from India slightly preceded that from Pakistan, while that from Bangladesh was even further behind. The peak period of arrival for west Indian-born persons living in Britain in 1987 was 1955-64, for the Indian- and Pakistani-born it was 1965-74 and for the Bangladeshi-born 1980-84. The gross movement from Bangladesh, perversely, shows a direct rather than a negative correlation with unemployment in Britain. It has been said that West Indians in Britain face an 'Irish' future while Asians face a 'Jewish' future.

By this it is implied that West Indians will remain concentrated in blue-collar occupations, council housing and with low educational qualifications, while Asians will move more to entrepreneurial activities and self-employment in white-collar jobs with owner occupation and higher educational certifi-cation. In Great Britain, during 1987-89, the Indian male occupational structure was very close to the white population and above it at the top end.

For example, 11 per cent of Indian men were in professional occupations compared with seven per cent for the white population; 19 per cent were employers or managers compared with 20 per cent for the white population and 16 per cent were in other non-manual occupations compared with 18 per cent for the white population. The comparable figures for the combined Pakistani-Bangladeshi population were five per cent, 16 per cent and 11 per cent respectively.

However, as with most generalisations, this hides many contrary examples. Perhaps, as far as the Asian population is concerned, the most serious qualification is that it hides major differences in housing tenure characteristics between the national origin groups.

The Indians and Pakistanis have the highest housing

tenure profile while the Bangladeshis are, in some ways, closer to the Caribbean model. Indian households were 77 per cent owner occupiers in Great Britain in 1983-85; Pakistani households were 74 per cent owner occupiers while the proportion for the white population was 59 per cent and that for Bangladeshi households, 35 per cent.

Recent estimates of the South Asian ethnic population of Britain is that Indians number 779,000, Pakistanis 433,000 and Bangladeshis 111,000. These figures include direct migrants from the subcontinent, secondary migrants from third countries, mainly East African, together with children born in the UK.

Of the Indian ethnic population 39 per cent had been born in India and 20 per cent in East Africa. About one per cent of the Pakistani ethnic population was East African born. Most East African Asians are classified as 'Indian' and roughly 20 per cent of the Indian ethnic population of the UK is East African in origin. One of the effects of the massive redistribution of world wealth in the aftermath of the 1973 petroleum price rise was the huge increase in demand for labour in the Gulf. The South Asian population in the Middle Eastern oil-rich countries grew from about half a million in 1975 to nearly two and a half million in 1985. The emerging ethnic and regional tensions in Nepal would be absorbed and accommodated with the demographic framework of polity but if not, then any outbreak of conflict on these divisive lines would produce refugees. India would be the only destination of these refugees, particularly from the Limbuwan region because of socio-cultural identities of Rais, Limbus, Magars and Gurungs across the border in India where there is concentration of Indian Nepalis in North Bengal and Sikkim. Democratic politics in Nepal promises to play a positive role in diffusing ethnic tensions by channellising them through political parties, media, non-governmental organisations and even parliament.

Communal and regional forces suffered serious setbacks at the 1991 and 1994 elections may not be underestimated. There is, however, no scope for complacency as some regions of Nepal are not free from regional and ethnic problems and similar developments in India tend to activist-sectarian identities which cut across national boundaries of the countries. Besides these potential conflicts becoming a source of refugees in South Asia, there are also prospects of economic migration increasing in the region in the years to come. This is because of the growing thrust of economic liberalisation and integration/harmonisation of regional economy encouraged by the post-Cold War international economic trends and the IMF/ World Bank-sponsored structural adjustment programmes.

According to UNHCR there is a return of 103,000 refugees from Pakistan to Afghanistan during 1994, even in the midst of reintensified conflict. This could be possible, perhaps because the fighting was confined mostly to Kabul and its vicinity, and the refugees belonging to other areas could go back. Similarly, the Bangladesh government, with the help of the UNHCR could help 82,860 Rohingyas go back to their villages in Myanmar during the later half of 1994. India succeeded in repatriating 8,150 Sri Lankan Tamils to Sri Lanka and 5,200 Buddhist Chakmas to Bangladesh during 1994.

In doing so, while India sought the good offices of the UNHCR in the case of Sri Lankan refugees, the repatriation of Chakmas was worked out on the basis of rehabilitation and financial incentives from the government of Bangladesh. India also managed to send back 'forcibly', nearly 2,000 Chin-Myanmar from Mizoram, where they were living in refugee-like circumstances. Since the mid-sixties, in the context of repatriation, there has been a significant shift in South Asia. Earlier there was a greater willingness to accept refugees and rehabilitate them without making efforts for their repatriation. This was clearly the case with regard to the refugees that crossed Indian and Pakistani borders in 1947 and later on.

Influx of Refugees

India also accepted refugees coming from Sri Lanka and Myanmar during the early sixties. The obvious reason behind India's responses was that during partition, it was accepted that the displaced people were the responsibility of the host country, notwithstanding the fact that India had not endorsed the two-nation theory that sought to divide states on the basis of religion. India, also, it seems had either accepted its moral responsibility or found it politically prudent in the aftermath of conflict with China to rehabilitate the refugees from Myanmar and Sri Lanka. India and other South Asian countries had also accepted refugees coming from Tibet since the early fifties, possibly, as a result of political decision to make use of them strategically in their relations with communist China. Gradually, the South Asian countries have become more and more unwilling to accept refugees coming from their neighbours.

Even when Pakistan has made a strategic use of the Afghan refugees and India of the East Pakistan and Sri Lankan refugees, the efforts have been to send them back soon after the strategic value of the refugees was lost and the burden of their presence became an economic, administrative and political liability. Now the shift in the global attitude towards the refugees, of "keeping would-be refugees at home" has also strengthened the South Asian attitudes, not only to resist the incoming refugees but also to send those living for a long time, back as soon as possible.

Almost every South Asian country—India, Pakistan, Bangladesh and Nepal—have even used force, either to stop refugees from coming, or to send them back, or in both the circumstances. UNHCR interventions and the pressures from various NGOs as well as refugee groups themselves have at times slowed down their repatriation not based on voluntary choice, but the hardened attitude that the refugees must return has continued. As a result of such attitude, refugees, like the Sri Lankan Tamils, have preferred to return and stay in the rehabilitation camps within their country, in the absence of propitious conditions in their traditional places of residence. The persisting conflicts in Sri Lanka and Afghanistan may be mentioned in this regard. Even refugees that have gone back, like the Sri Lankan refugees, have mostly remained confined to internal refugee camps, because their villages and towns are still the theatres of conflict and there is no immediate possibility of their destroyed homes and farms to be reconstructed or repaired. More so in the case of Afghan refugees where neither their own government, nor international relief agencies are in a position to be of much help.

For instance, under a bilateral agreement with India, the Bangladesh government promised "a 16-point repatriation and reintegration package that included financial assistance worth some $250" per individual, but on actual verification of conditions on ground, it was found that "less than half of the financial aid promised" had been given and other conditions had not been created for the repatriates to "settle in their places of origin".

South Asian countries have pursued various strategies and actions to deal with the refugee problems and their respective security implications. At the local level two broad patterns of settlement adopted for the refugees are evident in South Asia. The host state has either kept the refugees in well defined camps at one place or kept the movements of the refugees somewhat restricted.

Alternately, refugees have been dispersed to different areas, farther from their points of entry, and even among the local populations that do not share much of the socio-cultural identities with the asylum seekers. In such cases, refugees have also enjoyed a greater freedom of movement and activity, including seeking jobs and organising themselves politically. The settlements of Afghan refugees in Pakistan and the Tamils of Sri Lanka in India may be mentioned here. Security risks and instances of instability caused by tensions between the local population and the refugees have been the largest and the most severe in such cases. In relation to the external dimension of the refugee question, the general and most natural strategy adopted by the host state has been to engage the home state in direct negotiations to resolve, and/or moderate the implications of the refugee presence.

This strategy has been considerably successful in terms of its costs and results. Bilateral and negotiated agreements between India and Sri Lanka on the Tamil issue, the Myanmar and the Bangladeshi governments on the Rohingyas, and between India and Bangladesh on the Chakmas, may be mentioned in this regard. Such agreements have not been perfect and their implementation has often been tardy and cumbersome, resulting in slow and delayed resolution of the problem at hand.

In the cases where antagonism and incompatibility between the interests and objectives of the home and the host states are sharp and deep, this strategy may not yield the desired results. At times the benign influence of international agencies and the third parties like the UNHCR may help break the ice and facilitate the evolution of an agreement but this is not always the case. The case of the Bhutanese refugees in Nepal may be mentioned here. Bilateral negotiations have not yet shown signs of success, particularly because Bhutan is not even willing to accept the dimensions of the problem. But there lies no other better alternative than to continue to negotiate in the spirit of mutual accommodation and compromise. Similarly, Bangladesh has not even been willing to accept formally that there has been illegal migration of its nationals into India in search of economic opportunities.

Chakma Refugees

There is, however, an informal acceptance on the part of Bangladesh that the problem exists and that it should be resolved amicably. It may therefore be advisable that the two sides continue to discuss this question bilaterally. After all, consistent negotiations did produce positive results on the question of Chakma refugees.

The repatriation of Chakmas has been stalled due to the difficulties in the execution of promises on the part of Bangladesh, but this in no way reduces the importance of negotiations and accommodation. The failure of negotiations to resolve the refugee-generating conflicts has led South Asian states to try drastic strategies, involving armed hostilities, war and intervention. This was evident in India's approach to the problem of East Pakistan which eventually led to the emergence of Bangladesh in 1971.

The Indian military intervention in arming the Mukti Bahini, and fighting a full-scale war with Pakistan which enabled the ten million and odd refugees to return to Bangladesh was initiated after the failure of other options. The then Prime Minister of India, Indira Gandhi, had clearly warned that "Pakistan cannot be allowed to seek a solution of its political or other problems at the expense of India and on the Indian soil." The strategy of intervention and war was also evident in dealing with the crisis of Afghan refugees in Pakistan. The US, Western powers, their allies and China had all joined hands with Pakistan to force the Soviet military out of Afghanistan and thus create conditions for the return of refugees. The qualitative difference in this situation with that of the Bangladesh conflict of 1971 was that while the intervention and war in Afghanistan was a part of the global Cold War and Sino-Soviet rivalry, in the 1971 conflict the host state alone was motivated into action to defend its interests.

The burden of the global rivalries in fact lent support to the home state, Pakistan, in 1971. The third instance of this drastic strategy in dealing with the refugee-generating conflict in South Asia was India's intervention and pressure on Sri Lanka.

The Agreement of July 1987 aimed not only at securing conditions for the repatriation of refugees but also at resolving the ethnic conflict through a fair accommodation of Tamils' fights and interests. In all the instances of the use of war and intervention as strategy to deal with the refugee issue, we must reiterate that return of the refugees was only one of the many objectives and motivating factors. This involved political use of refugees by the host state in pursuance of broader and diverse interests. It may also be kept in mind that this strategy only partially resolved the refugee-related concerns.

The hopes of a very amicable relationship between India and Bangladesh also vanished after initial years when India started facing the pressure of economic and illegal migrants from Bangladesh. In Afghanistan, the arms and militia forces raised during the war of attrition precipitated yet another internecine conflict which has not allowed all the refugees to repatriate. In Sri Lanka, the 1987 Agreement and the political and military arrangements envisaged under this, ran into rough weather due to changing political dynamics in the two countries. The conflict in Sri Lanka has also been reintensified, leaving the unrepatriated refugees in the lurch. Besides the partial and constrained efficacy of the strategy of war and intervention, this option is also not available to all.

The weak and small countries are incapable of pursuing such a strategy either in relation to each other or *vis-a-vis* a strong and powerful neighbour. Thus a country like Nepal cannot take resort to this strategy either against Bhutan where negotiated solution does not hold much promise, at least for the time being, or against Tibet. Nepal is also not in a position to exercise pressure against India to stop the inflow of economic migrants.

There is a pressure for liberating SAARC from this disability of not discussing bilateral and contentious issues, particularly from countries like Pakistan, Bangladesh and Nepal. But this is a politically motivated pressure, not sincerely concerned with the resolution of problems and evolution of mutually accommodative solutions. Almost all the counties in South Asian are afflicted by the refugee problem and in some cases, the refugee issues affect more than two countries. The Bhutanese refugees, for instance, are an issue both in India and Nepal. The Bangladeshi economic and illegal immigrants are present in India, Nepal and also Pakistan. There are also Bihari Muslims in Bangladesh who have proclaimed their loyalties to Pakistan but have not been able to go to their cherished land. In addition, the security implications of refugee movements involve drug trafficking and terrorism, the areas which are already covered under a regional SAARC convention.

7

Women in Politics

The Assembly in the Maldives included women from the outset. In comparison to other nations in Asia, it was Mongolia which, by recognising the electoral rights of women as early as November 1924, stands out as a pioneer. It was not before the 1930s that things changed in Sri Lanka 1931, in Thailand and the Maldives 1932, in Burma, now Myanmar 1935 and in the Philippines 1937. Only after the Second World War did women in most other Asian countries gain the rights to vote and to stand for election. For instance, the People's Republic of China granted political rights to women on first October 1949, followed a few months later by India. Bangladesh, the last born of the independent states of the region, concluded the process on 4th November 1972, or nearly 50 years later and 12 years before Europe. Among the island states, in Tonga a woman was not elected to Parliament until 15 years after its inception and some 30 years after women were granted electoral rights.

According to the Constitution, most recently revised in January 1998, being male is a necessary qualification to be elected as the President or Vice-President of the country. Women have equal rights to vote and have the right to seek public representative office, except the office of the Head of State. The total number of eligible voters among women was lower than men by 6,688 in the November 1999 elections. However, they had a higher voter turnout percentage of 84.3 as compared with 71.2 for men, indicating widespread political awareness among women.

Women Representation

The first political party set up in the Maldives in the early

1950s consisted of 4,741 members of whom nearly one third were women. In the same party two women and three men were elected as honorary chairpersons. In addition, the advisory committee to the party consisted of three women and 13 men. Today, despite legislation, women's participation in the national political sphere and in leadership positions in the decision-making process is extremely low. The total number of elected women in the 1999 elections was two. Since there are also three other women among the eight nominated by the President, the total number of women MPs is now five, that is, five out of 50 or 10 per cent.

There has been a visible discrepancy between the increase in population and growth in the Maldivian labor force. Between 1985 and 1990, the labor force grew by only 1.5 per cent and there was a heavy reliance on expatriate labor from Sri Lanka, India, Pakistan and Bangladesh. This slow growth rate in the labor force is attributed to shifts in the age structure of the population to a larger proportion of younger men and women, lack of availability of trained personnel, and a relative decline in the number of working women. The atoll female Labor Force Participation Rate (LFPR) fell from 72 per cent in 1977 to 20 per cent in 1990. During the same period, the LFPR, which declined only marginally for males from 25 per cent to 22 per cent between 1985 and 1990, was less steep and more evident in the atolls. Subsequently, the LFPR has been increasing for women but has not touched the 1977 levels. This decline has been mainly due to the reduction in the women's traditional involvement in fish-preservation (dry fish) activities as a result of the mechanisation of the fishing industry and the export of raw rather than dried fish, as also because of limited opportunities for higher education. Although there are no restrictions on women's right to receive higher education, the lack of safe and convenient hostel facilities has hindered girls from joining educational institutions in far-off islands. Women have also been unable to benefit from the boom in the tourism industry due to certain economic and geographical factors and because the industry offers no provision for the families of workers to live on the resort islands.

The trend of women's reduced LFPR began to reverse after the advent of the 1990s when the setting up of several garment industries offered women some increased opportunities for joining the labor force. The higher proportion of the workers continues to be from neighboring countries. The decline in women's LFPR is particularly evident in the atolls and therefore any analysis of this trend must dissociate the situation of the women in male from their counterparts in the far-off islands, where agriculture and fishing are the main sectors for female employment. Employment opportunities for women have not kept pace with development in the country, with women from the islands being particularly disadvantaged. Women on the atolls continue to have large families and spend most of their time at home, caring for their families while the men leave their homes for fishing, or migrate to the other islands for employment. In some atolls, one half of the households are headed by female members.

Women are, however, more involved in the traditional but unpaid tasks of community life such as the education of their children in traditional or religious schools, sweeping the island, beaching dhonis (Maldivian boats), cooking meals or preparing food for community events. There are few avenues for wage employment on the islands. In male where women have greater access to wage employment, in all likelihood, they bear the double burden of work both inside and outside the home. Facilities such as child-care services that support women's participation in employment are absent.

Socio-economic Changes

Socio-economic changes in the islands have also reinforced the segregation of tasks between the sexes and exacerbated inequalities between them. Women traditionally processed the fish caught by the men, producing 'Maldives fish' that was recognised as a delicacy, especially in Sri Lanka. When the 'Maldives fish' formed the main merchandise export of the country, the LFPR of women was over 50 per cent which, at the time, was one of the highest in the developing world. The modernisation of the fishing industry has enhanced opportunities for men, motivating them to increase their catch and sell it to collection vessels. The fish is subsequently exported in frozen form or processed at the canning factory. These developments have significantly curtailed opportunities for women to engage in fish processing and, as a result, their

LFPR in economic activity declined to 21 per cent in 1985, falling further to 19 per cent in 1996.

Today the Maldives has one of the lowest rates of economic participation by females in the world. Women appear to be working as unpaid family labourers rather than as paid workers with cash income. The rapid growth of the Maldivian tourism industry has significantly increased employment opportunities for men, but not yet for women and families. The work requires men to move to and live on the resort islands away from their families and home islands. Maldivian women, on the other hand, have resisted work for which they would have to travel away from their homes because of continuing traditional beliefs about the role of women, and culturally induced fears of women's exposure to moral danger or external influences that are inconsistent with the prevailing cultural and religious mores. In 1996 of the nearly 5,000 Maldivians employed in the tourism sector, less than 100 were women.

Workers Overseas

The men working overseas or in male remit most of their incomes to their home islands, which has further reduced the need for women to earn independent incomes. The rise in household incomes brought about by the growth of tourism has contributed to a decline in the traditional cottage and handicraft industries, in some of which women traditionally participated. Another factor that has contributed to a decline in women's LFPR has been the lack of opportunities to continue their education beyond the primary or secondary level. Accordingly, they tend to marry and begin their families shortly after finishing school.

New Developments

New developments in the industry such as the establishment of canning and garment factories have provided limited opportunities for Maldivian women in the workforce, despite special transport arrangements being made for them to travel to the workplace. For example, at the tuna-canning factory in Felivaru, only 30 women are employed from the neighboring islands as against more than 100 women from Sri Lanka.

The willingness of Sri Lankan female workers to work longer hours for lower wages has also allowed them to dominate the garments sector. In recognition of the low LFPR of island women in economic activities, the National Development Plan had recommended implementation of programs for the economic empowerment of women with the aim of enhancing the women's decision-making abilities and promoting their access to assets and resources.

However, these programs often serve to reinforce their domestic roles rather than creating job opportunities for them in the growth sectors. While there are no exact figures for underemployment, the 1998 Vulnerability and Poverty Assessmcnt estimated that the potential labor force in the Maldives has been underestimated by at least 10 per cent and that approximately one third of the country's labour force can be estimated to be underemployed.

There are very few women in high positions in the Government at present. Traditionally women were mostly involved in child rearing and domestic activities until recently. For this reason, very few women joined the workforce and worked their way up to senior positions. However, things started changing a little when English education was introduced in the Maldives in the 1960s in both government schools (Majeediyya School for boys and Aminiya School for girls).

Opportunities were given to boys and girls to complete Grade X and appear for the GCE O-Level exams of the University of London Schools Examination Board. But this opportunity was not available in the island schools. There was thus a migration of students to male from the other islands to pursue higher studies in these two government schools. As more boys than girls completed Grade X, they found employment in the government and private sectors. Very few students, and that too mostly boys, were able to go abroad for higher education.

Although there is an increase in the number of women who do manage to secure good secondary education and get tertiary education from overseas universities and colleges, women still face certain problems that prevent them from devoting long hours in the workplace and hence competing with men to attain higher posts in the government and private sectors. Women still have to take care of their families and children.

The traditional system of grandparents and extended family members looking after the children is no longer practically possible as they too have joined the workforce. Baby-sitting and child care are thus real problems faced by working mothers today, especially in male which comprises over one third of the total Maldivian population. However, it is encouraging to note that husband and wife teams have started working together to take care of their children, thus replacing the women in their traditional child care roles. This is more prevalent in couples who are in their 30s or younger still, where one or both partners might have had the benefit of a good education. The income poverty line for the Maldives, that is, the cut-off point for the availability of adequate cash for basic household needs, has been defined to start at Rf600 (US$51). According to this definition, 40 per cent of the rural population falls below the income poverty line. About 15 per cent of the population is estimated to subsist with an income of Rf75 per day or less. The 1998 Vulnerability and Poverty Assessment has estimated the annual average household monetary income to be Rf1,300-1,800 (US$68-111). Nearly 25 per cent of the most impoverished population is found to live on the 19 islands of the Republic.

Dependency on imported foodstuffs, uncontrolled market prices for most foods and an inflation rate of 7.6 in 1997 have lowered the purchasing power of many households. The consumption of fruits and vegetables is confined to the higher income group of the urban population. It is estimated that 6 per cent of the population suffered due to a food crisis during the previous year. The Assessment indicated that 22 per cent of the country's population has a daily income of less than Rf10 (equivalent to US$0.84). Nearly all the people falling in this category reside in the outer islands. It also revealed that the average daily income for the male region is estimated to be three times that of the outer atolls, indicating that the benefits of development have not reached the majority of the population. Vulnerability as measured by access to the economic and social infrastructure was found to be highest in the small and distant islands. However, there is an emerging urban poor class in Male, which faces severe constraints of space and livelihood. While organised child labor is nonexistent in Maldives, there has been recent anecdotal evidence of the exploitation of island children, particularly girls, who have been studying in male and living with families as part-time domestic labor. Although the average marriage age is rising, particularly in the larger and more developed islands, many Maldivians marry at a very young age, often as young as 15 years. Registration of marriages and divorces is mandatory. Arranged marriages, though prevalent earlier, are no longer popular, Under *Shari'ah* law, men are allowed to marry more than one woman but the man may not be married to more than four wives at any one time. All wives must be treated equally and the man must possess means to look after his multiple wives and their children. There is however, a declining trend in men following this practice. According to the 1995 Census, only one in 11 of all men were married to more than one woman at the time of the Census. Traditionally marriages were arranged until about 50 years back. Today most people in the Maldives choose their own marriage partners. However, parental consent is very important. Since the Maldives is a 100 per cent Muslim country, the bridegroom has to ask the bride's father for his daughter's hand in marriage and this is essential for the Islamic marriage ceremony. Divorce is also simple and grounds for obtaining divorce are simpler for husbands. The current high rates of divorce and multiple marriages are a cause for great concern, particularly due to the impact of this phenomena on the fertility rates of women. Some estimates place the divorce rate as high as 75 per cent of all marriages registered.

Girls and women will have a legal guardian, normally the father, no matter how old they are. If he is not alive, then the grandfather; if he is not alive, then a brother who should be more than 15 years in age; if the brother is younger than 15, then an uncle, etc. These stipulations are in accordance with the laws of Islam. A man, thus, has in principle more legal responsibilities towards his family. Women, like men, have a right to their own property, whether they are married or not. According to Islamic *Shari'ah* a man inherits twice as much as a woman. However, the man is obliged to care for his family as well as provide for his wife and children and whoever is in his guardianship such as younger sisters, aunts, nieces or nephews. A woman does not have such legal obligations.

In Islam divorce is said to be the last resort in case a marriage fails, after having tried to resolve differences over a period of time. But the high incidence of remarriage among the same couples indicates that divorce is not operating as it should be, that is, as the last resort.

There are seminars and media campaigns at government and community levels to strengthen family bonds, for instance, the new Family Bill passed by the People's *Majlis* and ratified by the President in 2000, which will come into effect as of 1 July 2001. It is hoped that this would have a positive impact on the family system and reduce divorce rates. Divorced women often face very difficult problems, trying to raise young children and managing a job to earn a living. This becomes even more difficult if they do not have a supportive family. In such situations, if men give support and maintenance to their children as they are supposed to do, according to the laws of Islam, then the children would not have to face any hardships. But in practice, a large proportion of women are faced with the burden of bringing up a family on their own without much financial support from their ex-husbands. Now there are government programs to ensure that men carry out their family obligations to their children.

There are no strong stigmas attached to divorced women; divorced women have an equal chance as men for remarriage. It is not uncommon for women to have a better marriage the second time round. Remarriage is very common in the Maldives. It is quite normal for children of both partners from their previous marriages to live as an extended family. But this poses many problems, such as the children sometimes finding it difficult to accept a step-parent as a parental figure. Premarital sex is prohibited in Islam for both men and women. Extra-nuptial births bring great shame to the family and are punishable by law. The girls or women involved are always punished for this crime, but the man involved can only be punished if he confesses and claims paternity or if there are four witnesses (which is highly unlikely). Fortunately, such girls are not ostracised by family or society.

The only systematic current enumeration of female-headed households was found in the report of the 1998 Vulnerability and Poverty Assessment. The definition of a female-headed household adopted by the assessment was not confined to a household in which the wife of mother is without a husband as a consequence of death, desertion or divorce. It was defined more broadly in terms of the person regarded by household members as being the head of the household. Overall, around one in three of all households are headed by a woman. Variations were evidenced between atolls, with the percentage of female-headed households reaching around one half of all households in some cases. Interestingly, no major differences were found between male and the atolls and three out of four women replied that their position as head of household was based on their desire to be in-charge. Female household heads when asked to enumerate the main hardships they encountered grouped them into three main areas: financial difficulties and problems of generating an income along with household responsibilities, child-rearing obligations, and difficulties in fulfilling roles traditionally played by men. No major difficulties or hardships were reported by a large number of women with regard to management of the household.

Planning for the development of women has evolved gradually in the Maldives. The country has not witnessed a strong women's movement as in some of the neighboring countries because gender equity appears to be a part of the Maldivian psyche and is in line with the global evidence of greater equity among the island populations.

However, it must be recognised that gender is not a static concept and it varies from region to region and changes over time. While government policies for the advancement of women have been intrinsic to the development plans of the country, the actual translation of these has evolved slowly and perhaps needs a greater thrust with the changing economic scenario.The Government is committed to broadening the role of women and their effective participation in all aspects of society. A National Policy on Women (NPW) was formulated in 1996 through a process of wide-ranging consultations at all levels throughout the country. Implementation of the policy is one of the objectives of the Fifth National Plan, 1997-2000. The goal of the policy is to achieve a socially and morally justified partnership of women and men in human-centered development on the basis of equity and social justice.

The NPW covers a wide range of areas: health, education, economy, media, politics, leadership and legislation. This policy document will be implemented via the National Plan of Action on Women in Development (NPAWID). The establishment of a formal machinery for women's affairs can be traced to 1979 in response to the need to prepare for the International Decade for Women.

A Preparatory Committee for the International Decade was set up under the National Planning Agency. It was renamed the National Women's Committee in 1981 and acted as a focal point for women's development directly under the office of the President. In 1986 the Committee was renamed as the National Women's Council and acts as the advisory body to MWASS.The Office for Women's Affairs was created in 1986. Three years later it was upgraded to be a full-fledged Department of Women's Affairs, functioning directly under the Office of the President.

The Department of Women's Affairs was responsible for facilitating and organising programs for social and economic development of and to strengthen their capacity to enable full participation in mainstream national development. Further upgradation to a ministerial level followed with the establishment of the Ministry of Youth, Women's Affairs and Sports (MYWAS) in 1993.

More reshuffling of portfolios in 1996 resulted in the setting up of the current incarnation of the Ministry for Women's Affairs and Social Welfare (MWASW). In 1998, the name of this Ministry was further changed to Ministry of Women's Affairs and Social Security (MWASS). MWASS consists of four sections, namely, the administrative and budget section; the social security section; the unit for the rights of children, and the women's section. The National Women's Council was dissolved in December 2000 with the establishment of the GEC. The mandate of the GEC is as follows:

i) Guide and advise MWASS on issues for which help is sought;
ii) Incorporate women's development programs into

national development programs;

iii) Promote gender equality to ensure that women and men benefit equally from national development;

iv) Advise MWASS on measures to eliminate gender discrimination and violation of women's rights;

v) Assist MWASS whenever and wherever required;

vi) Represent the Maldives at different national and international forums should MWASS request the GEC to do so;

vii) Advise and assist MWASS on follow-up actions of international/regional action plans on gender equality; and

viii) Conduct networking among the members of the National Women's Council with a view to enhancing the gender component in their respective ministries.

IWCs were established on 1 January 1993, by the National Women's Council under a recommendation of the Second National Conference on Women. They were established in inhabited islands to increase women's participation in community activities and national development, in addition to the ward committees, which were established on 8 October 1982. These committees are semi-NGOs working under the guidance of MWASS. The members of the IWCs consist of women elected from the island community. The island chief is the advisor to the committee.

There are 215 IWCs altogether. Some IWCs are well organised and have successfully involved women in activities related to the social development of the island such as the construction of women's mosques, schools and health centres and the renovation of school buildings. Economic development projects have proved less successful. It has been reported that women sometimes are not clearly aware of the purpose of IWCs or that they were seen as a means to increase women's participation in island and atoll development projects. In one survey, women expressed a desire to play a wider role in community activities but were unable to articulate how this could be achieved. In 1989, UNICEF initiated a program of building women's development centres in the islands. Thus now there are 11 women's centres opened and another three to be opened in the coming years. Ten of these were established by 2000.

The women's development centres are built on specific islands, which have neither a health centre nor a hospital, in addition to inhabiting a population of more than a certain number. Furthermore, the islands were chosen in consultation with the atoll administration and the atoll chiefs. Once the island is chosen, the construction of the centre is the responsibility of the islanders. Materials required were provided by MWASS.The main objectives of these centres are to provide a hygienic environment during childbirth and to serve as a place for the island women's committees to carry out their development activities.

Status of Women in Maldives Under Specific CEDAW Articles

Convention Article 1: Definition of Discrimination

Paragraph 13 in Chapter II of the amended Maldivian Constitution, states that "Maldivian citizens are equal before and under the law and are entitled to the equal protection]and Phrases." The definition of law includes government practices as well as "norms and provisions of Shari'ah established by the Noble Quran and the traditions of the Noble Prophet, and the rules derived therefrom."Therefore, discriminatory treatment of women is justified by attribution to Shari'ah or interpretations of it.

Convention Article 2-5: Traditions, Stereotypes and Obligations to Eliminate Discrimination

Severe restriction on freedom of religion in the Maldives has a critical impact on the enjoyment of women's human rights. Over 99 percent of all Maldivians are Sunni Muslim, and the public expression or practice of any other belief system is strictly prohibited. Recently, two women who were suspected of practicing another religion were detained for several months. Also, Buddha pictures belonging to a UN expert were confiscated. This association of religion and government has led to a powerful system of media censorship. The government owns and runs all radio and television stations. Freedom of expression is strictly limited by governmental policy.

Women are directly affected by the restrictive culture. They do the vast majority of household chores and cooking, tasks which reportedly take many women almost the whole day. In the capital, Male, the numerous responsibilities women have in the home are made more difficult by the shortage of space, since economic factors have led to a highly concentrated population. An average of 14 people and three families live in each small home with no yard. Working conditions in homes are often dark and undesirable.

The Australian Agency for International Development has described the situation as follows: "The poverty that exists in the Maldives disproportionately impacts on women due to social and cultural restrictions on their mobility: women are not as free as men to travel outside of their home atoll (island district) unaccompanied. Educational and employment opportunities, as well as access to services, are more limited in these areas."

Convention Article 6: Trafficking in Women and Prostitution

The Maldives, as a member of the South Asian Association Regional Cooperation (SAARC), has participated in a number of conferences and workshops in the past few years addressing the problem of trafficking of women and children in and from South Asian countries. Maldives hosted the 9th SAARC Summit, which resulted in the Male Declaration on trafficking. This is commendable, but it is unclear what effect these efforts have had on reducing the practice of trafficking. Trafficking is still a problem in the Maldives. In May 2000, Sri Lankan police began a search for a Russian man who they believe controls Russian prostitutes in Maldives and other SAARC countries.

Convention Article 7: Political and Public Life

The President, Cabinet Ministers and members of the People's Majlis (Parliament) are required to be Sunni Muslim and to observe Shari'ah (Islamic law). Women are not allowed to run for president. They may hold other public positions, but very few do. Three women have served in the Majis (parliament) and one woman has served as a cabinet member.

Currently, male clerics dominate the most post powerful positions in the Maldivian government. It has not always been so. Before Islam was embraced in the islands, several islands enjoyed varying levels of matriarchal leadership.

Nevertheless, under the current system, both women and men are entitled to vote, as long as they are Muslim and at least 21 years of age. Statistics on voter turnout disaggregated by sex were not available, though the Government allowed a team from the SAARC observe the 1994 elections.

The practice of keeping tourists and native Maldivians primarily on separate islands is intended to minimize the adverse effects of tourism on the traditional Muslim communities. This policy of privacy also keeps hidden information on women's participation in public life.

Convention Article 9: Nationality

The Maldivian Constitution states, "No Maldivian shall be deprived of citizenship except as may be provided by law." Converts to other religions may lose their citizenship, thought the Government claims this provision has never been applied.

In 1998, two Maldivian women were arrested and imprisoned for over three months for converting to another faith. They did not lose their citizenship, but the length of their imprisonment indicates that their conversion was viewed as a threat to national stability. Though dozens of men and women were questioned on this occasion about converting, only the two women were imprisoned and counseled extensively. Human Rights Without Frontiers reported that religious prisoners in Maldives are pressured to deny their faith.

Convention Article 10: Education

Men and women enjoy equally high literacy rates (93%), especially in comparison with neighboring Asian countries. A high percentage of boys and girls attend primary school. At secondary levels, though, the gap favoring education for boys increases rapidly. Though there is no national legislation that restricts equal access to education, NGOs claim that social customs and norms foster the gap. Often, parents refuse to allow their girls to attend school past 7th grade when there is no secondary school on their home island.

Many girls stay at home to help with household tasks socially assigned to women. Many others leave school to bear and raise children. Sixty-five percent of Maldivian women marry before they are 18.

Convention Article 11: Employment

Culture dictates a certain level of separation of men and women in the workplace. Women are found in lower-paying positions, such as clerical work, agriculture, and service jobs in the tourist sector. This is especially true of the foreign women working in Maldives. In 1999, the Bangladesh National Women Lawyers Association discovered that 27 female migrant workers had not been paid wages for three years of work in Maldives. Women who do work outside of the home are still expected to manage and clean the home.

Though widespread poverty affects all Maldivians, women are hit especially hard. Because the Maldives has the highest divorce rate in the world, overburdened mothers have become the rule rather than the exception. Women are underrepresented in the workforce. IPPF reports that 78 percent of men are in the workforce, compared to 43 percent of women. Another source reports that only 18 percent of women are in the workforce.

Maldives has experienced rapid economic growth and modernization over the past decade, but many women benefit less from this growth, because some traditional beliefs conflict with women's free participation in the economic market.

Convention Article 12: Health Care and Reproductive Rights

Health is probably the most urgent problem facing women in the Maldives. Only about 75 percent of the population have access to health care. The World Health Organization (WHO) and the Society for Health Education (SHE), a local NGO, have worked to provide education and training resources regarding general and reproductive health. Despite their efforts, maternal and infant mortality rates remain high. Twenty percent of live births result in low birthweight babies. Anemia is found in approximately 68 percent of pregnant women, 62 percent of non-pregnant women, and 82 percent of children.

Statistics on access to safe water are unclear. Safe water is widely available on tourist resort islands, but it is somewhat irrelevant to include this access in national statistics, because few Maldivians live on tourist islands. Ground water in the Maldives is contaminated and the islands suffer from water shortages in the dry season.

There is little training or counsel for mothers, especially regarding their health and the health of their children. Women are generally not trained in the benefits of breastfeeding, even though low breast-feeding rate is one of the factors responsible for deficiencies in children, such as Vitamin A Deficiency (VAD). Only eight percent of Maldivian mothers breastfeed their newborn children exclusively. Maldives has not adopted the international code on marketing breast milk substitutes.

Poor feeding practices are responsible, according to WHO, for the malnutrition of children in Maldives. Severe malnutrition has not decreased since 1985. Growth monitoring of children up to three years old is common practice, but though 38 percent of children under five are underweight or suffer from wasting or stunted growth, "no attempts are made by the health workers to take special care or counsel the mothers." There are some efforts to combat these problems, but systematic and complete data on progress made was unavailable.

Poor nutrition is so critical because the associated health problems reproduce at an alarming rate. The birth rate is high, averaging about six children per woman. WHO stated, "High population growth is threatening the quality of life, especially of women and children." About half of the population is under 15 years. Distribution and availability of contraception is limited and requires a prescription. Only 15 percent of women between 15 and 49 reported using contraception of any kind. Reported contraception use rates remain extremely low, despite family planning training programs for family health workers. There is widespread male reluctance to use contraception, especially condoms.

In summary, International Planned Parenthood Federation (IPPF) reports, "Early marriage. . ., frequent pregnancies, chronic malnutrition and inadequate health care services jeopardize safe motherhood in the Maldives."

Another health problem that persists because of inadequate (reproductive) health services is Thalassaemia. Twenty percent of the population carries this fatal genetic blood disorder and one in 250 children develop the actual condition. A child of two carriers has a 25 percent chance of being born with the disease. Those with the disease suffer from anemia and must undergo monthly blood transfusions and daily injections. The only cure is a bone marrow transplant, which is costly. SHE provides free screening and counseling, but the effect of its services on the frequency of the disease is unknown. The IPPF commented, "Unless something is done to decrease the numbers born with the illness, the amount of clean blood and bone marrow to go around is likely to become a commodity reserved for the rich."

Convention Article 14: Rural Women

Not only is the population of the Maldives concentrated in Male, the wealth is as well. Poverty is especially harsh in the outer atolls. Infant and maternal death rates are even worse in rural areas, where the small population lives in isolation, often without sufficient access to health care facilities, education, and employment. On some islands, only half of the children reach adulthood. Because contraception is only available with a prescription at a few health care facilities, most rural women have no access to it.

Convention Article 15: Equality before the Law

A woman's testimony is equal to one-half of a man's in court cases involving finance and inheritance. Courts handling matrimonial and criminal cases do not allow legal counsel. This may pose problems for women who are unaware of their rights. Also, male heirs get twice the inheritance of female heirs.

Convention Article 16: Marriage and Family Law

Women and men both have the freedom to select a spouse. This "freedom" is allowed because of the population's ideological homogeneity. Men, however, may marry up to four wives under Islamic law.

Divorce is available to men and women, but husbands may divorce more easily if the decision is not mutual. Women marry an average of four times. It is common for Maldivians to divorce three to six times. Women suffer greater losses in divorce than men do, because of their financial dependence on their husbands.

Women often stay in the homes of their ex-husbands until they remarry, especially since the population has exploded in Male, with 30,000 inhabitants per square kilometer. The effect on women and children of being forced to continue residence with an estranged husband or father has not been closely addressed.

General Recommendation No. 19: Violence Against Women

Domestic abuse is a problem in the Maldives, despite a cultural norm against aggression. Though statistics are unavailable, one health counselor reports, "There are a lot of cases of sexually abused children, and there will be many unreported cases also. It is mostly girls who are abused; in fact, all my cases of sexual abuse have been with girls." Incest is also a problem for girls and young women, exacerbated by crowded living conditions, where many residents sleep in the same room.

The SHE has tried to curb this through education programs. The organization counsels victims of sexual abuse by telephone and in person. However, organizational resource are stretched thin, and most attention goes to the other fundamental deficiencies in women's physical and mental health care.

Women's rights advocates agree that wife beating and other forms of violence are not widespread. There are no firm data on the extent of violence against women because of the value attached to privacy in this conservative society.

In 1997 the Government commissioned a study by a local nongovernmental organization (NGO) on domestic violence, but it was never completed. Police officials report that they receive few complaints of assaults against women. Rape and other violent crimes against women are extremely rare. None were reported or prosecuted during the year. Under Shari'a the penalty would be flogging, banishment, or imprisonment for up to 5 years.

Women traditionally have played a subordinate role in society, although they now participate in public life in growing numbers and gradually are participating at higher levels. Women constitute 38 percent of government employees, and about 10 percent of uniformed NSS personnel. Well-educated women maintain that cultural norms, not the law, inhibit women's education and career choices.

In many instances, education for girls is curtailed after the seventh grade, largely because parents do not allow girls to leave their home island for an island having a secondary school. Nonetheless, women enjoy a higher literacy rate than men. Due largely to orthodox Islamic training, there is a strong strain of conservative sentiment—especially among small businessmen and residents of the outer islands—that opposes an active role for women outside the home. However, the Government continued legal literacy programs to make women aware of their legal rights and workshops on gender and political awareness in the outer atolls.

The Government also has built 10 of 15 planned women's centers in the atolls, which are facilities where family health workers can provide medical services. The centers also provide libraries and space for meetings and other activities with a focus of the development of women.

Under Islamic practice, husbands may divorce their wives more easily than vice versa, absent any mutual agreement to divorce. Islamic law also governs intestate inheritance, granting male heirs twice the share of female heirs.

A woman's testimony is equal to only one-half of that of a man in matters involving adultery, finance, and inheritance. Women who work for wages receive pay equal to that of men in the same positions.

In October the Cabinet replaced the National Women's Council with a Gender Equality Council to serve as an advisory body to the Government to help strengthen the role of women in society and to help ensure equal participation by women in the country's development. Also during the year, the Government, with the assistance of the European Union and the U.N. Population Fund, expanded a program of small loans to women for development projects to additional islands.

The Government does not have a program of compulsory education, but it provides universal access to free primary education. The percentage of school-age children actually in school was as follows: (grades 1 to 5) 99.26 percent, (grades 6 to 7) 96.2 percent, and grades (8 to 10) 51.09 percent. Of the students enrolled, 49 percent are female and 51 percent are male.

The Government is committed to the protection of children's rights and welfare. The Government is working with UNICEF to implement the rights provided for in the U.N.

Convention on the Rights of the Child. The Government established a National Council for the Protection of the Rights of the Child in 1992. Government policy provides for equal access to educational and health programs for both male and female children. Laws protecting children's rights apply with equal force to children of either sex.

Children's rights are incorporated into law, which specifically protects them from both physical and psychological abuse, including abuse at the hands of teachers or parents.

The Ministry of Women's Affairs and Social Welfare has the authority to enforce this law, takes its responsibility seriously, and has received strong popular support for its efforts. The Ministry noted an increase in reports of child abuse during the first part of the year with 138 reports involving 317 children, including 10 reports of sexual abuse. Penalties could be banishment or imprisonment for up to 3 years. It is not known if there were any prosecutions during the year. The Government is reviewing the law to see if improvements and additional protections are necessary. There is no reported societal pattern of abuse directed against children.

8

The Assessment

The Finding on the basic Rights have been Dealt with in a Comprehensive Way

This report is submitted in accordance with the Convention on the Rights of the Child (1989) to which Maldives is a party, and it contains a brief overview of the activities carried out by way of implementing the said Convention in Maldives.

Maldives has made considerable progress in enhancing the situation of children (and women), particularly in child survival and basic education. All attempts are being made to improve the condition and status of the girl child, to reduce maternal mortality, to ensure safe motherhood, and to provide quality and equity of early childhood development and primary education, nutrition and access of safe water and sanitation to maximum levels achievable within the constraints of the physical structure, infrastructure and available resources of Maldives. There exists firm political will to foster such improvement and structural frameworks within which to do so.

General Measures of Implementation

Maldives is an Islamic nation of long-standing and, in keeping with the Islamic tradition of ensuring sound upbringing of children, the welfare of children has always been a priority in the country. It was among the very first countries to ratify the historic Convention on the Rights of the Child. The practical activities that were subsequently undertaken in the country were a manifestation of Maldives commitment to the Convention, and to children.

The Government of Maldives under the leadership of His Excellency President Maumoon Abdul Gayoom is committed to fulfilling the needs of children, to safeguarding their basic human rights; to ensuring their right to enjoy the benefits of social and economic progress of the society and to guaranteeing a safe environment for them as emphasized by the Convention on the Rights of the Child, the World Declaration on the Survival, Protection and Development of Children and the decisions of the South Asian Association for Regional Cooperation (SAARC) Summits (1986-1991).

The fact that almost 50 per cent of the Maldivian population is comprised of children under 16 years of age, calls for even greater attention to promoting the total well-being of children. It is to this end that the activities specified in the Convention are being implemented.

The first such activity was declaring 1991 as the Year of the Maldivian Child. One of the most significant events of the year was the National Conference on the Maldivian Child, held in Malé, the capital of Maldives, from 8 to 11 July 1991.

The Conference highlighted the situation of Maldivian children and formulated measures to achieve their well-being in the light of the recommendations and global strategies adopted by the World Summit for Children, held in 1990. It adopted the Declaration on the Survival, Protection and Development of the Maldivian Child and an inter-ministerial coordination committee prepared the National Programme of Action (NPA) for achieving the goals set.

In November 1991, The Law on the Protection of the Rights of the Child was passed (Law 9/91). This was the first major piece of legislation passed subsequent to ratification and, following the content of the Convention, represented a landmark by recognizing the rights of children and their freedom and dignity and aiming to create conditions in which they can develop their full potential and look forward to a full and satisfying adult life. The Law initially identifies guiding principles and objectives for the State, parents, and the community in respect of their responsibilities towards children in endeavouring to make children patriotic, religious and healthy with a good upbringing.

This Law is the main legal document on children's rights

and is the framework on which the implementation of the Convention is based. It states that any person in contempt of this law can be jailed, banished, placed under house arrest or fined. The Ministries responsible for each section are, over time, developing practices and specific policies, which can then be enforced through the use of the sanctions identified.

As a follow-up, the National Council for the Protection of the Rights of the Child was established, its mandate being to observe the role of the State, parents and the community and to monitor the goals set in the NPA. The establishment of a central database to monitor those goals is currently under way with the collaboration of the respective parties.

The National Council for the Protection of the Rights of the Child is headed by the Minister of Home Affairs, as the chair. The National Council is composed of 15 members from 12 different bodies, which include the Ministries of Health and Welfare, Education, Justice and Islamic Affairs, Youth/ Women's Affairs and Sport, Atolls Administration, Planning and Environment, Defence and National Security, Information and Culture, and Home Affairs. Also represented are the Attorney General's Office, and the Maldivian Parliament.

A special Unit for the Rights of the Child (URC) was established at the Ministry of Home Affairs on 1 November 1992. This was seen as a major outcome of the efforts made to improve the welfare of children. The unit deals with all issues related to children's rights, their publicity, promotion and implementation. A primary task of the Unit is to offer a counselling service to children (and parents) whose behaviour is problematic, either at home, at school or in the community; and to children who have been abused, abandoned or neglected.

The number of cases reported to the Unit is suggestive of the fact that children face many problems that warrant attention.

An analysis of these cases suggests that the underlying causes of child-related problems are associated with social issues such as broken families and changing societal values that are challenging traditional values and causing a rift between generations.

To offer a unified national service to the country's

children URC has commenced a programme of training for personnel in the atolls. To date, training programmes have been run in Fuah Mulah and Ari Atoll. There are a further four training workshops planned for 1996.

Training needs are high both amongst the URC counsellors, who, whilst highly committed and motivated, are young, unqualified and with little experience, and amongst the volunteer counsellors, in Malé and on the atolls.

URC has been financially assisted by UNICEF since its inception in 1992, and in 1995 Voluntary Service Overseas (UK) posted a volunteer as Child Rights Coordinator, primarily to train counsellors in Malé and throughout the country.

General Constraints on Development

An almost unique environmental constraint to universal and sustainable development in Maldives is the physical structure of the country. The people of Maldives inhabit 199 out of a total of over 1,190 coral islands, widely dispersed over a large area. The dispersed and fragmented geographic nature of the country is reflected in every aspect of life and exerts a dominant influence on the infrastructure (as infrastructure costs would need to be replicated over most of the 200 islands) and, consequently, on the ability and opportunity to develop, fully, equity of services for children throughout the country.

The capital island, Malé is populated by nearly one quarter of the total population of the country, which currently stands at about 245,000. The remaining population is sparsely distributed among the 199 inhabited islands. Economic concentration around Malé (and the tourist resorts) has led to internal migration and a flow of resources resulting in widening disparities within the country, despite an overall improvement of economic conditions. Decentralization, which is conducive to sustainable development is being pursued.

Environment degradation related to fresh water aquifer depletion, saline water intrusion in the fresh water aquifer, solid waste management and disposal, coral mining, land reclamation destroying reefs and coastal erosion, and global warming leading to rising sea levels (the latter, in fact, threatening the security of the whole nation) seriously impede development.

A further threat to the environment is the population

expansion, Maldives having one of the highest population growth rates in the world. A growth rate of 3.5 per cent threatens to undermine the quality of life, particularly in the atolls. Population and ecological balance is hindered by depletion of vegetation, fuelwood, water supplies, coral and sand (for construction). Elements of population policy have been included since 1988 in the National Development Plan which brought about progress in population programmes in the atolls. 1995, however saw the emergence of an extensive population policy, dealing with a whole range of issues connected with family welfare, under the management of the World Health Organization (WHO).

Because of the rapid population increase, the number of children to be served by the main services, i.e. health and education, multiply quickly, exerting pressure on existing facilities and leaving little time for forward planning.

Whilst transport facilities have improved recently (through the mechanization of dhonis, increased air transport and harbour deepening), transport between islands and atolls remains difficult.

Public information

The Convention on the Rights of the Child has been translated into the Maldivian language, Dhivehi. To date, one thousand copies have been distributed to the public by URC. A simplified version of the Convention has been included in a report published by URC, which also includes a descriptive, statistical and analytical report on the cases reported to URC.

Section 7 of the Law on the Protection of the Rights of the Child specifies that special programmes imparting information and advice relevant to children, should be telecast/broadcast through television and radio. This section also indicates that the programmes targeting children should not use undesirable language or scenes which might have a negative impact on the behaviour of the child. In this regard, Television Maldives and the Voice of Maldives broadcast special programmes for children. Some of the programmes are presented by children themselves. Special columns in the daily newspapers are allocated to children.

Furthermore, some of the programmes broadcast through television and radio are intended to inform the general public about the upbringing of children, reminding parents and making them more aware of their duties and responsibilities towards their children. In these programmes due reference is made to Islamic values and principles relating to the development of the child. URC also plays a continuing role in raising public awareness of child related issues, through the production of posters and leaflets on a regular basis.

Definition of the Child

The Law on the Protection of the Rights of the Child (Law No. 9/91) defines any person below the age of 16 years as a child. The age of attainment of adulthood is, however, 21 years. Legal minimum ages established for specific purposes include:

- Legal/medical counselling without parental consent, 16 years;
- Education, whilst not compulsory, is encouraged up to the age of 16 years; Sexual consent is forbidden outside of marriage;
- There is an unwritten rule that marriage before the age of 15 should be prohibited and, under Law 9/91, section 21, parents are advised to discourage marriage before the age of 16. Early marriages continue to occur in Maldives, particularly in the outlying atolls;
- Voluntary enlistment into the National Security Services can only be made by those over 16 years old;
- Children under 16 years cannot give testimony in court;
- Regarding criminal liability, Maldivian law regards a person over 15 years as criminally responsible. Children under 15 are not charged with offences, unless the offence is murder, use and trafficking of drugs, major theft and fornication or religious offences;
- The Law on the Protection of the Rights of the Child (Law No. 9/91) prohibits any child who is below 16 years being employed, for gain, at a place where persons are employed for gain; The Rules of Procedure of the Courts require that children below the age of 16 shall not be subjected to imprisonment or banishment;
- Consumption of intoxicating substances and/or drugs is forbidden to all Muslim persons.

General Principles

Non-discrimination (art 2)

It is provided in the Maldivian Constitution that all persons are equal before the law and that equal rights are guaranteed to men and women.

Stereotyping of gender roles results in the girl child from infancy of parental expectations of roles associated with childbearing and child rearing. Simultaneously, the boy learns to assume a role of financial caretaker of the family based on the role model provided to him by his father and other male relatives.

The traditional, predominating role of women is that of wife and mother and a pervasive feature of Maldivian society, particularly in the outlying atolls is that women marry very early, remarry several times and bear a number of children, from a very young age until their mid-forties. This has serious implications for their health. This situation is, however on the decline, as can be seen in Malé, where women comprise around 50 per cent of the workforce, some of them occupying prestigious positions.

Best interests of the child (art. 3)

In making decisions regarding custody it is emphasized that all parties concerned should ensure that the best interests of the child are served.

Children under 7 years will, primarily, remain with their mother. If this is not deemed appropriate (if, for example, the mother is to remarry and have other children), custody will be offered to the maternal grandmother, the paternal grandmother or the father, in descending order of priority. Children over the age of 7 years can choose in whose custody they wish to remain.

Right to life, survival and development (art. 6)

Law 9/91 (chap. 1, No. 2) states that "provision should be made to ensure maternal and child health from the time of conception to delivery, through health education of parents, and the treatment of illnesses".

Under Maldivian law, the definition of a child commences at the time of conception. It is, therefore an offence to abort the child at any stage of a pregnancy. Pregnancies can only be terminated if there are serious medical reasons which threaten the health of the mother.

Section 4 of Law 9/91 requires the Government to identify reasons for child mortality, and aims to reduce it by raising public awareness. This Law reinforced action taken in 1990, when the World Summit for Children was signed by the President. This approved a Plan of Action whose goals included:

– Reduction of the infant mortality rate, by 50 per 1,000 or one third, whichever is less;
– Reduction of the under-5 mortality rate by 70 per 1,000 or one third, whichever is less.
– The present infant mortality rate stands at 30 per 1,000 live births (Statistical Year Book).

Respect for the views of the child (art. 12)

In custody cases involving children, the views of the child are given considerable weight by the courts. Upon reaching the age of 7, the child has the right to opt in whose custody he would remain.

Civil Rights and Freedoms

Name and nationality (art. 7)

Section 2 of the Law on Vital Registration at birth (Law 7/92), requires that an application be made to register the birth of a child within seven days of the date of the birth. Under the said Law it is the responsibility of the father and, in the absence of the father, of the mother to file such application. Failure to do so would result in a fine.

The citizenship laws of Maldives have been amended to enable a child whose father is a foreigner and whose mother is Maldivian to apply for Maldivian citizenship.

Preservation of identity (art. 8)

The Law on Registration of Births and Deaths further requires that an application be made for a certificate of registration of the child before the child reaches the age of 16 years. Children can only attend school if they are registered, so compliance is high.

Freedom of expression (art. 13)

The Constitution of Maldives guarantees freedom of

expression to all its citizens. Since children fall within the definition of citizens, they too enjoy the same rights in respect of freedom of expression. This would include freedom to seek, receive and impart information and ideas of all kinds in writing or in print or through any other media of the child's choice.

Access to appropriate information (art. 17)

The Law on the Protection of the Rights of the Child, No. 9/91 (chap. 1, No. 7) states that special programmes consisting of information necessary for children should be broadcast and that the programmes should not consist of materials which are injurious to the child's well-being.

To enable children to have access to information and material from a diversity of national sources, a section of the National Library specially caters for children's books, magazines and materials. National radio and television (introduced in 1978) disseminates information and materials of social and cultural benefit to the child by way of children's programmes. Law No. 9/91 expressly prohibits dissemination of any information that is detrimental to the dignity of the child.

Freedom of thought, conscience and religion (art.14)

As Maldives is a 100 per cent Muslim country, the Constitution of Maldives is silent about the freedom of religion. Regulations do, however, permit non-Muslims to practise their religion in privacy. Thought and conscience are inextricably bound by and linked in Maldives with the Muslim religion, which all Maldivian citizens must follows and practise.

Freedom of association and peaceful assembly (art. 15)

Freedom to assemble without arms is a fundamental right entrenched in the Maldivian Constitution. Children enjoy the same rights that any other Maldivian citizen enjoys.

Protection of privacy (art. 16)

The Constitution provides legislation to guarantee the privacy of individuals, including that of children.

The right not to be subjected to torture or other cruel, inhuman or degrading treatment or punishment (art. 37)

The Law on the Protection of the Rights of the Child (Law No. 9/91) prohibits imposing cruel and degrading punishment on children. New legislation was enacted in 1991 which considers those under the age of 16 as children and provides for special consideration in the prosecution and punishment of juvenile offenders.

Section 18 of Law 9/91 prohibits the beating of children, or imposing severe punishment which might harm the child mentally or physically, by parents. It is not an accepted form of child punishment. Section 10 of Law 9/91 aims to ensure that punishment in school will not affect the child physically or psychologically.

Family Environment and Alternative Care

Within Maldivian society, it is common to find a very high rate of marriage, divorce and remarriage. Most women are married by 18 years of age and remarried four to six times by the time they are 50. One consequence of these "multiple" marriages is that some children are likely to have one or more step-parents (in addition to their natural parents), half-siblings and, consequently, large and complex kinship networks. One type of extended family which exists is "polynuclear", which clearly has advantages in terms of the greater variety of relations with whom the child can identify and form relationships, and greater opportunities for alternative care arrangements.

The extended family is, traditionally, the norm, a newly married couple taking up residence with the family of one of the partners. Consequently, households are quite large (particularly on Malé owing to the limitations on living space) and may have a number of different generations residing together.

Parental guidance (art. 5)/Parental responsibilities (art. 18)

Sections 13 to 15 of the Law on the Protection of the Child deals with parental responsibilities, rights and duties. These sections cover the parents' responsibilities for the upbringing and development of the child, including their duty to provide shelter, food, clothing and basic health care for their child and the obligation to give them basic education.

Parental responsibilities towards children are, inevitably, affected by the high rate of divorce. In the traditional society, within the extended family, divorce meant no major disadvantage to the child or the parents. Children were mostly taken care of by another member of the family. Basic needs were met rather modestly in the subsistence economy, so the financial burden was not felt. Today, however, (particularly in Malé) some children and women in divorced families are not cushioned by extended families. These children are felt to be children in especially difficult circumstances in the context of Maldives. The number is increasing, particularly urban adolescent children without adequate space to live, children from poor families, children of broken families, school drop-outs and those without adequate parental care, all particularly vulnerable to turning to crime. There is growing public concern that a law and order problem is emerging in Malé, with fears of youths spending time on the streets, forming gangs and getting involved in substance abuse.

To ensure that the child is afforded legal protection from matrimonial disharmony and separation, Law 9/91 (chap. 2, No. 19) states: "if parents have to separate this should not affect the child's education, conduct or health".

Separation from parents (art. 9)

The extended family supports children who need to be separated from their parents. There is a residential institution, exclusively for boys. Further services and facilities are planned to be developed.

Children may face separation from one or both parents because of the high incidence of divorce; and children from some atolls leaving their own families to "lodge" with friends or relatives elsewhere for the duration of their studies.

Family reunification (art. 10)

Maldives has not experienced situations such as armed conflict, civil wars or social unrest, so there is no legislation or policies on this issue.

Recovery of maintenance for the child (art. 27)

Law 9/91 (chap. 2, No. 20) states that if parents are divorced or separated, support should be provided for the children in accordance with court orders.

Children deprived of a family environment (art. 20)

Section 11 of Law 9/91 gives importance to protecting the rights of orphans. In the absence of parents or legal guardians, the Government should ensure the development of institutions, facilities and services for the care of these children.

The Unit for the Rights of Children is involved in all cases of neglect or abandonment. Residential care is provided by the Ministry of Education at the Maafushi Education and Training Centre, which accepts boys between the ages of 9 and 16. There are no provisions for girls. Extended families tend to provide alternative care, in the absence of the natural parents.

Adoption (art. 21)

There is no "formalized" system of adoption in Maldives, although the system that does operate is organized through the Ministry of Justice and Islamic Affairs.

Illicit transfer and non-return (art. 11)

Not being subject to wars, internal conflicts or political instability, the application of this article in Maldives is felt to be unnecessary.

Abuse and neglect (art. 19, including physical and psychological recovery and social integration (art. 39)

Section 25 of Law 9/91 prohibits all forms of physical or psychological violence, injury or abuse, neglect or negligent treatment or exploitation, including sexual abuse.

The Unit for the Rights of Children deals with all reported cases of abuse or neglect. The Unit is based in Malé, and residents of Malé can be guaranteed the offer of counselling to help to reintegrate victims back into families/ communities, if appropriate, or to offer suitable support. In the atolls, however, there are few trained counsellors and the opportunities for receiving formal counselling is therefore limited. Maafushi Education and Training Centre is used to accommodate boys who are neglected, but only with the consent of their parents.

Periodic review of placements

Cases of children placed in the Maafushi Centre are reviewed on a regular basis, with the intention of assessing their suitability to return home. Placements are agreed between URC and the island offices, the atoll offices, the Ministry of Education, Maafushi staff and the parents, all of whom have a role in reviewing progress. Annual return home for a month ensures that all boys who have families have the opportunity to renew family relationships, and test their ability to remain in the family environment.

Basic Health and Welfare

Survival and development (art. 6)

Antenatal care is available to all pregnant women, primarily through the family health worker and the "foolhumaa" (traditional birth attendant). Although inadequate maternal care, difficulties in transporting the women to hospital, either in Malé or to the regional hospitals, and chronic undernutrition continue to make delivery and motherhood risky, significant improvements have taken place over the past decade.

Indicators of child survival and development are the infant mortality rate and the under-5 mortality rate. (See para. 35 above.) Law 9/91 (chap. 1, No. 4) states the need to find the cause of infant mortality and to reduce it through a programme of health education. There has been a sharp reduction in the infant mortality rate and the under-5 mortality rate, first in Malé and then in the atolls, as a result of a number of improvements.

Maldives has achieved universal child immunization against the six main vaccine-preventable diseases of childhood, with a coverage of over 90 per cent. Other common morbidities include: Viral Hepatitis B, which presented a high incidence in the Maldivian population. A vaccine against Hepatitis B was added to the immunization schedule in 1993; Thalassaemia a fatal congenital condition affecting 1 in 250 children born and resulting in an average life span of four to five years. In order to reduce its incidence, the National Thalassaemia Programme and a Public Awareness Programme are run by the Society for Health Education (SHE), a non-governmental organization, including screening and counselling services in the community and in secondary schools. The National Thalassaemia Centre was opened in 1994 to address the problem. Diarrhoea continues to be endemic in Maldives, particularly in children under 5, due to lack of awareness of proper hygiene. There has been a reduction in diarrhoeal mortality, through mobile teams promoting Oral Rehydration Treatment too. Acute respiratory infection is the largest single cause of child mortality and morbidity and is a major health problem. The NPA calls for its reduction by launching a programme for screening, upgrading diagnostic skills and public education.

These developments have brought about a significant reduction in the infant mortality rate, which in 1993 stood at 34 per 1,000.

There is also a nation-wide programme to educate mothers concerning the proper upbringing of children. Apart from regular radio and television programmes, leaflets and posters are published and distributed freely on this subject. In this programme, special emphasis is laid on the physical, mental and emotional development of the child.

Disabled children (art. 23)

Law 9/91 (chap. 1, No. 6) places responsibility on the Government to provide "any possible assistance, depending on resources and facilities to minimize physical disabilities".

Law 9/91 (chap. 2, No. 17) places responsibilities on the parents in respect of disabled children: "If a child becomes disabled, the special needs of the child should be fulfilled, taking into account the financial resources of the parents. The child should be prepared for employment and recreation, in order to achieve the fullest possible social integration and individual development."

Disabled children do not appear to have been a major concern in Maldivian society, perhaps as they were traditionally taken care of by their families.

A special programme for primary-aged blind and deaf children is conducted in a regular school in Malé, with a specialist teacher in charge.

Health and health services (art. 24)

The Ministry of Health and Welfare is responsible for the provision of health services. They consist of: Indira Gandhi Memorial Hospital (the central referral hospital), Malé; Malé Health Centre; 4 regional hospitals; 22 community health centres at atoll level; and 212 health posts (1993). The Indira Gandhi Memorial Hospital is the best equipped, providing certain specialist medical care for the whole country. There are also a number of private health clinics in Malé, which are proving a popular choice. More complicated conditions are treated abroad.

Community health centres, with community health workers provide primary health care. Community health workers visit islands once every two months to deliver medicines and contraceptives and supervise the work of the family health workers (FHWs). The health post, manned by an FHW, is the basic preventive health care (not curative) available on the islands. On some islands there is only a "foolhuma". Efforts are under way to staff every health post by an FHW and a "foolhuma".

Despite recent expansion, the health service faces major constraints:

– Difficulties in recruiting and retaining staff at all levels, due to shortage of suitable candidates;
– Inadequate and basic training;
– Inadequate diagnostic capabilities.

Several health projects have been launched with the assistance of UNICEF, and UNFPA is supporting health studies and assisting Society for Health Education (the only NGO involved in an ongoing project).

Government expenditure on health has substantially increased in recent years. The NDP 1991-1993 provided for a 6 per cent annual growth in resources allocated to health.

Since the country cannot cope with a booming population, there is a nationwide programme to promote and increase the availability of family planning services, through the Department of Public Health, UNFPA and SHE. Small families are encouraged with a view to improving the standard of living. However, despite these efforts, only around 23 per cent of currently married women are contraceptive users. A host of institutional and sociocultural factors affect the implementation of an efficient delivery service with an outreach to island women.

Social security and child care services and facilities (arts. 26 and 18)

There are no national laws regarding social security or insurance.

There are few child care services or facilities. The demand for them may appear, to some, to be limited, because large, extended families can offer greater opportunities for family members to provide care to young children if both parents are working. However, with traditional extended families now being replaced by smaller, "nuclear" families, the demand for child-care provision will become more obvious.

Standard of living (art. 27)

Nutrition

To improve the standard of living of the child, information on nutritious food is disseminated through the media and also by distributing leaflets. Despite such campaigns, undernutrition remains widespread, with around 50 per cent of children suffering ailments related to unbalanced diets. Such chronic undernutrition results in short physical stature, or "stunting" (estimated around 30 per cent), underweight for age, "wasting" (estimated around 40 per cent), low birth weights and poor child health.

There are, however no severe cases in Maldives. The reasons for undernutrition are:

- Inappropriate weaning;
- Lack of knowledge of nutrition and care practices;
- Occasional shortages of a variety of foods on some of the isolated islands;
- Lack of diversity and adequacy of food intake;
- Diarrhoea;
- Worm infestations.

Iron deficiency is a problem in Maldives. Some 30 per cent of children are believed to be suffering from anaemia. It is a major public health problem, currently being tackled by raising awareness concerning health and nutrition, and improving antenatal care. Sanitation/safe water.

Maldives Water Supply and Sanitation Authority (MWSA) is responsible for overseeing all water supply and sanitation activities throughout the country. In the 1980s the Maldives Government initiated action and made progress in providing safe drinking water and sanitation. Providing universal access to these two basic needs still remains a major challenge. The NPA pledges to:

- Maintain universal access to safe water in Malé;
- Raise rural access to safe water from 50 per cent (1990) to 80 per cent by 1995 and to universal access by 2000;
- Maintain universal access to sanitary latrines in Malé;

– Raise rural access to sanitary latrines from 22 per cent (the current level) to 25 per cent by 1995 and 50 per cent by 2000.

Water supply

Drinking water is either rainwater or well water, except in Malé where desalinated water is available. MWSA is currently installing pipes throughout Malé, to provide piped, desalinated water to each household. Rainwater is safe but varies in quantity. Well water varies widely in quality. Access to safe water is therefore dependant on a number of variables. The number of people with access to safe water will be low until the number of rainwater tanks is increased. The collection of rainwater is, however, dependant on roof surface area, and in some areas this is not sufficiently high to provide enough water. MWSA has also commenced a programme of installing rainwater tanks on the outlying islands.

Constraints

The hydrogeological characteristics of the small islands pose problems of obtaining safe drinking water for a population that has been rapidly expanding and thereby depleting groundwater faster than it is being replenished. Other constraints are:

(i) MWSA is a centralized organization with limited manpower;
(ii) Construction of storage tanks for harvesting rainwater is problematic because of lack of skills, lack of site location and the high costs of underground storage;
(iii) Desalination of seawater is too costly;
(iv) Importing and storing water is too costly.

Sanitation

Traditional systems of "gifili" (digging pits) and defecation on the beach pose health hazards for all islands except for a few large ones with small populations. Provision of safe latrines has been problematic: the flush toilet system does not suit Maldivian conditions as it promotes the discharge of the limited groundwater into the sea. Alternatives have been tried with little success, most having met with a high degree of social unacceptability.

Like safe water, sanitation facilities are fully maintained

in Malé, where sewerage service is provided to almost all households. However, in more than half of the islands outside of Malé water and sanitation problems have become the main concern. The overwhelming demand is for private modern latrines and public sewerage systems that have no long-term negative effect on the environment, are acceptable to the people and are affordable.

Housing

Housing plots are allocated free by the Government, but there is a wide disparity of housing quality between Malé and other islands. On Malé there is very limited space, insufficient for the population; consequently there is a selection procedure for applicants for building plots, leaving others reliant on expensive rented accommodation.

Male "houses" around 61,250 people (one quarter of the country's population), on an island just under 2 sq. kms. in size. This makes it one of the most densely inhabited capitals of the world. Accommodation is very scarce, resulting in high rents and small dwellings, with little or no private outside areas. As families tend to be large and multi-generational, and dwellings small, overcrowding is a common and often acute problem. Many households live in constant lack of privacy and space.

Although some other islands do have areas of high population density, overcrowding is relatively rare outside of Malé. Families elsewhere enjoy much larger dwellings, with much more space both inside and outside for children to play.

Education, Leisure and Cultural Activities

Section 5 of Law 9/91 lays down government responsibilities to provide facilities for education and personal development in all the islands, depending on the resources available. In this manner, religious teachings should be highlighted. Also, recreational facilities should be provided.

Section 15 of Law 9/91 lays down parental responsibilities as ensuring children's right to education, religious education and an upbringing to the best of the parents' financial capabilities.

Education (art. 28)

The national education system is currently a mix of

traditional institutions (Edhuruge's, Kiyavaage's, Makthab's and Madhurasa's) and modern schools, although the former, traditional system is being slowly assimilated into the modern system. The primary education system is a five-year cycle which children enter at age 6. The sixth and seventh year is the Middle School and is part of the seven-year extended basic education, which defines the minimum educational attainment for all children by the year 2000.

Grades 8, 9 and 10 compose lower secondary education, at the end of which students can take, 0-Levels. Lower secondary schooling, grades 7 and 8, was previously only available in Malé, but has now been introduced on several other atolls. Upper secondary education, grades 11 and 12, is offered only at the coeducational Science Education Centre in Malé. There is no tertiary education in the country. The Non-Formal Education Department provides educational and vocational training courses, both within Malé and, on a distance learning basis, for children on the outlying islands.

Schooling is provided free in the government schools (although there are also private institutions) and, whilst it is not compulsory in law, children are encouraged to attend school until the age of 16, and more than 95 per cent of primary-school-aged children are enrolled in a school. The primary education programme constituted one of the major campaigns between 1980 and 1990. People have thus begun to realize the importance of an education, if not their right to one, and 1 in 3 of the country's 245,000 people currently attends school.

Many of the problems relating to education stem from the dispersed and fragmented physical structure of the country. Providing the facilities, teachers and learning materials that high quality schooling requires in all the 200 inhabited islands is not possible. The solution that has been developed is to concentrate educational resources, especially above the primary level, in Malé. Children seeking education at higher levels have to leave their home island to attend school in Malé. This has resulted in inequity in educational quality between Malé and the atolls and pressure on existing facilities necessitating shorter school hours and multiple sessions on a "shift" system. The highest level of education achieved in

Maldives is year 12, and further studies have to be undertaken abroad. The total number of graduates is a little over 300. This lack of skilled personnel hampers development.

Aims of education (art. 29)

The aim of education in Maldives is to develop children mentally, physically, emotionally and spiritually in conformity with Islam. The ultimate objective is to produce responsible, understanding, cultured and industrious citizens who will enhance the country's development. The new "modern" system aims at developing a modern curriculum reflecting primarily the realities of the culture of the country and at the same time helping the country enter the modern world.

Leisure, recreation and cultural activities (art. 31)

Each academic year is comprised of about 190 days so children have plenty of time for recreation etc. Most schools have playgrounds and other facilities for sports and co-curricular activities are incorporated in the school curriculum. Schools organize and hold several sports events. Other activities like scouting, guiding, cadeting and music are common. Competitions are occasionally organized by NGOs too.

There are, on Male and several other islands, parks and recreational areas specifically for children. Various cultural activities are taught to children.

Special Protection Measures

Refugee children (art. 22) and children in armed conflict (art. 38/39)

Natural disasters of a devastating magnitude, war and famine have never occurred in Maldives and there are, therefore, no refugee children or children involved in armed conflict. There is, consequently, no legislation relating to such matters.

The administration of juvenile justice (art. 40)

Rules relating to the administration of juvenile justice are contained in the Penal Code (1960), the Law on the Protection of the Rights of the Child (2.12.91), and circulars issued by the Presidential Office and the Ministry of Justice.

Presidential decree No. 67/90 directs government authorities not to charge persons under 15 years of age for offences, stating that "small children" (up to 15 years) will suffer from psychological problems if they are prosecuted, taken to court and punished. The National Security Services (law enforcement agency) would refer to the child (under 16 years) to the Unit for the Rights of the Child (URC) who, following an initial assessment, will decide whether ongoing counselling is to be offered, in an attempt to "reform" that person. Additionally, parents would be summoned to the offices to sign documents agreeing to look after, and attempt correction of, the child and, if property were damaged or lost, to make compensation.

However there are exceptions, related to the commission of very serious crime, which in Maldivian law includes homicide, adultery, drug abuse and major theft. Every child, over the age of 7 years, who commits one of these offences is prosecuted and faces court proceedings and punishment. Presidential decree 67/90 instructs that such cases be closed appropriately by such authorities, by house arrest, so far as it is permitted by law.

Robbery, disloyalty and stealing also attract special attention, under Ministry of Justice Circular 4/88 (6.4.88), and children under 16 years of age face prosecution and punishment for these crimes. Punishment is dictated as house arrest for a period of not more than one year.

Children deprived of their liberty, including any form of detention, imprisonment or placement in custodial settings (art. 37)

The Law for the Protection of the Rights of the Child (9/91) prohibits imposing cruel and degrading punishment on children. Additionally, Ministry of Justice Circular 4/88 (6.4.88) and Presidential Administrative Directive 1-F/21/88/62 prohibit any child under the age of 16 being banished or imprisoned as they may "suffer serious psychological damage which may influence their future". It is required that such offenders be put under house arrest or fined in appropriate cases.

The sentencing of juveniles, in particular the prohibition of capital punishment and life imprisonment (art. 37)

Ministry of Justice Circular 4/88 (6.4.88) prohibits banishment and imprisonment for children under the age of 16 years.

Section 7 of the Penal Code states that save for the offence of murder or religious offences, the judge has the discretion to give lighter sentences.

Physical and psychological recovery and social reintegration (art. 39)

The Unit for the Rights of the Child and the Maafushi Training and Educating Centre provide rehabilitative services to juvenile offenders.

Economic exploitation, including child labour (art.32)

Law 9/91 (chap. 3, No. 27) prohibits any child under the age of 16 from working for payment.

In Maldives, unlike many other South Asian countries, child labour is not apparent nor widespread. Children are not hired as employees in any sector of the economy in any part of the country.

Drug abuse (art. 33)

Drug abuse is considered to be one of the most serious crimes and, under Ministry of Justice, Circular 2/924, (22.2.94), people under the age of 16 are prosecuted and face court proceedings. They cannot be sent to prison, but can be placed under house arrest for a period of not more than five years. Such legislation would seem to be in the interests and for the protection of the child as, if children were exempt from prosecution for drugs offences, the opportunity for adults to exploit children by utilizing them for the trafficking and sale of illicit drugs would increase. The legislation specifies severe punishment for persons who sell or give narcotic drugs to children under the age of 16.

There is growing concern about the number of cases of drug abuse, as incidents reported to the URC have increased. Drugs which are abused include those normally only available on prescription, such as tranquilizers, and illicit drugs such as marijuana, amphetamines and heroin.

Young people involved in substance abuse, and known cases will be referred to the URC for counselling. However, a Drug Rehabilitation Centre is shortly to open, which will accommodate both adults and children.

Sexual exploitation and sexual abuse (art. 34)

Section 25 of Law 9/91 places responsibility on the

community to report cases of maltreatment, sexual abuse or anything that affects a child's dignity, for judicial involvement.

The existence/incidence of child prostitutes is not known, and is certainly not evident. There have, however, been cases of sexual abuse referred to the URC although this may not reflect the full extent of abuse because there is, as in many countries, unwillingness to accept some forms of sexual abuse/ exploitation.

Sale, trafficking and abduction (art. 35)

This has not been an issue in Maldives, so legislation for its prevention is not felt to be necessary.

Other forms of exploitation (art. 36)

No other form of exploitation is evident or apparent in Maldives, so no additional legislation is necessary.

Children belonging to a minority or indigenous group

There are no distinct ethnic or minority groups in Maldives. Although traces of the old nobility still survive, intermarriage among all ranks of society is common. In Maldivian society no particular group is disadvantaged by lineage or place of birth.

Bibliography

Asian Development Bank, Maldives: *Human Development Issues for the 21st Century*, August 1999.

Bunch, Charlotte, "Women's Rights is Human Rights: Toward a ReVision of Human Rights." *Human Rights Quarterly* 12, 1990.

El-Solh, C.F. and Mabro, J., (eds.), *Muslim Women's Choices: Religious Belief and Social Reality*, Providence: Berg, 1994.

Maldives: *Country Operational Strategy Study*, 5 December 1995.

____________, *National Human Development Report*, First Draft, July 2000

Mallick, Ross, *Development, Ethnicity and Human Rights in South Asia*, New Delhi: Sage Publicaitons,1998.

Maloney, Clarence, People of the Maldive Islands. Madras, Orient Longman, 1980.

Mernissi, F., *The Veil and the Male Elite: A Feminist Interpretation of Women's Rights in Islam*, Translated by Mary Jo Lakeland. Reading, Massachusetts: Addison-Wesley, 1991.

Ministry of Health, *The Maldives Health Report*, 1999.

Ministry of Planning, Human Resources and Environment (MPHRE), *Fifth National Development Plan* 1997-2000, Vols. I and 11,1998.

Miralao and Ibrahim, "Women's Status and Development Trends", *A Survey Report*, October, 1991.

Moser, Caroline O.N., Gender Planning in the Third World: Meeting Practical and Strategic Gender Needs, *World Development*, Vol. 17, No.11,1989.

Omran, A.R., *Family Planning in the Legacy of Islam*. London and New York: Routledge,1992.

UNDP, Republic of Maldives, 1999.

UNESCO, *The Status of Women in the Maldives*, 1987.

World Bank, The South Asia Regional Gender Action Plan. Washington, D.C.,1997.

World Health Organization, "Women's Status in the Maldives", *Trends from Secondary Data Sources*, April, 1999.

Index